"Whosoever Will"

"Whosoever Will"

by

HERMAN HOEKSEMA

REFORMED FREE PUBLISHING ASSOCIATION
Grand Rapids, Michigan
(Distributed by Kregel Publications)

Library of Congress Catalog Card No. 77-189070
ISBN 0-916206-04-1

First Edition 1945. Reprinted 1972,
1973, 1977, 1980.

PRINTED IN THE UNITED STATES OF AMERICA

PREFACE

As the title of this book may suggest to those that understand, the following pages are intended to set forth the inseparable connection between the certainty that "whosoever will may come," and the truth of God's sovereign grace: the former is based on and rooted in the latter. That it may please the God of our salvation to use this book as a means to comfort those that come to Jesus, to strengthen the weak, to instruct the simple, and to establish those that are tossed to and fro by many winds of doctrine, is the prayer of the author.

H. HOEKSEMA

TABLE OF CONTENTS

Whosoever Will May Come

I

Whosoever Will May Come

And whosoever will, let him take the
water of life freely. —Rev. 22:17b.

WE are, no doubt, all acquainted with the hymn, the chorus of which runs as follows:

"Whosoever will may come.
Whosoever will, whosoever will;
Send the proclamation over vale and hill;
'Tis a loving Father calls the wand'rer home:
Whosoever will may come."

And you have probably guessed that with this hymn in mind I chose my general theme for the following chapters.

Definite reasons I have for doing so, and in elaborating upon this theme, I have a definite purpose in mind.

First of all, it has been my experience more than once that, when I preach the pure truth of sovereign grace, the gospel that salvation is of the Lord and in no sense of man, there are those who, as the children on the market place of which our Lord speaks, will pipe this hymn to me, evidently convinced that the words of it contradict and overthrow the doctrine that God sovereignly saves whomsoever He wills, and the will of man does not at all cooperate in his own salvation; and evidently intending that to the tune of their piping I shall perform an Arminian dance. And seeing that I hate all Arminian jazz music, that proudly extols the free will of the sinner, and could not possibly dance to the tune of it; considering, moreover, that it is my sincere desire to warn believers against the danger of the error that would attribute salvation to the choice of the sinner's will, and to instruct them in the truth of salvation by the sovereign grace of God, I feel that it might be beneficial and instructive to take the theme of the hymn and expound it in the light of Scripture: "Whosoever will may come."

This would not be proper, of course, if the theme were not a Scriptural one. It would hardly be safe to take the words of a man-made hymn as the basis for a positive discussion and presentation of the truth of the gospel. Many a hymn has served and still serves as a medium to instill false doctrine into the hearts and minds of those that sing them. But with respect to the particular hymn that bears the title "Whosoever Will" it may be said that its words are almost literally taken from Scripture, and that, therefore, no Christian can have any objection to it, provided it is properly understood, and interpreted in connection with the rest of the doctrine concerning salvation by grace. The words of it are probably in part taken from Rev. 22:19, where we read: "And the Spirit and the bride say, Come. And let him that is athirst come. And whosoever will, let him take the water of life freely." Moreover, the same truth is repeatedly expressed in Holy Writ in different forms. In Isa. 55:1-3 we read: "Ho, every one that thirsteth, come ye to the waters, and he that hath no money; come ye, buy, and eat; yea, come, buy wine and milk without money and without price.

Wherefore do ye spend money for that which is not bread? and your labor for that which satisfieth not? Hearken diligently unto me, and eat that which is good, and let your soul delight itself in fatness. Incline your ear, and come unto me: hear, and your soul shall live; and I will make an everlasting covenant with you, even the sure mercies of David." To those who complain that they pine away in their sins, and that, therefore, there is no hope of life for them, the Lord declares: "As I live, saith the Lord God, I have no pleasure in the death of the wicked; but that the wicked turn from his way and live: turn ye, turn ye from your evil ways; for why will ye die, O house of Israel? Ezek. 33:11. The Lord assures us: "Ask, and it shall be given you; seek, and ye shall find; knock, and it shall be opened unto you: For every one that asketh receiveth; and he that seeketh findeth; and to him that knocketh it shall be opened." Matt. 7:7, 8. And He sends forth the call promiscuously: "Come unto me, all ye that labor and are heavy laden, and I will give you rest." Matt. 11:28. "For God so loved the world, that he gave his only begotten Son, that whosoever believeth in him should not perish, but have everlasting life." John 3:16. And on the great day of the feast of tabernacles in Jerusalem He cried out: "If any man thirsts, let him come unto me and drink."

To be sure, then, the theme of the hymn is a biblical on. Whosoever is athirst may drink, whosoever is hungry may eat, whosoever is in need may ask, and he will receive; whosoever desires salvation may seek, and he shall find; whosoever is weary and burdened may come to Jesus for rest: whosoever will may come!

But I do object most strenuously to the singing of this hymn with the avowed or hidden purpose to gainsay and overthrow the doctrine of salvation by sovereign grace alone. Neither the words of the hymn, still less the text from Rev. 22:19 to which they, evidently, refer; nor any of the other passages quoted, can be used for this purpose. For that would mean that it were possible to appeal to one part of Scripture in order to refute another part, a possibility which may never be granted. For Scripture is the written record of the revelation of the living God through Christ Jesus our Lord. And as God is one, and Christ is one, so the Bible is one. It cannot contradict itself. And if anyone sings or preaches on the theme "Whosoever will may come" in such a way that the words are expounded as a denial of the truth of God's sovereign grace, he is simply distorting the meaning of the words.

Let us recall, briefly, what is implied in the truth of salvation through the free and sovereign grace of God alone. It means, in general, that God is the sovereign Lord, also in the matter of salvation. Salvation is, from its beginning to its end, a mighty wonderwork of God, no less marvelous, and therefore, no less divine, than the work of creation. It is that wonderwork of the Almighty by which He calls light out of darkness, righteousness out of unrighteousness, everlasting glory out of deepest shame, immortality out of death, heaven out of hell! It is the wonder of grace, whereby God lifts an accursed world out of the depth of its misery into the glory of His heavenly kingdom and covenant. That work is absolutely divine. Man has no part in it, and cannot possibly cooperate with God in his own salvation. In no sense of the word, and at no stage of the work, does salvation depend upon the will or work of man, or wait for the determination of his will. In fact, the sinner is of himself neither capable nor willing to receive that salvation. On the contrary, all he can do and will is to oppose, to resist his own salvation with all the determination of his sinful heart. But God ordained, and prepared this salvation with absolutely sovereign freedom for His own, His chosen ones alone, and upon them He bestows it, not because they seek and desire it, but in spite of the fact that they never will it, and because He is stronger than man, and overcomes the hardest heart and the most stubborn will of the sinner. He reconciles the sinner unto Himself; He justifies him and gives him the faith in Christ; He delivers him from the power and dominion of sin, and sanctifies him; He preserves him. All this belongs to the wonder of salvation, which is accomplished through sovereign grace alone.

Now there can be no doubt about the fact that the same Bible that repeatedly emphasizes in many ways that "whosoever will may come," also teaches very emphatically that the salvation of the sinner never and in no sense depends on the will of the sinner to come, but only on the sovereign will of God who is the Lord. "For whom he did foreknow, he also did predestinate to be conformed to the image of his Son, that he might be the firstborn among many brethren. Moreover whom he did predestinate, them he also called: and whom he called, them he also justified: and whom he justified, them he also glorified." Rom. 8:29, 30. Do not overlook the fact that in these verses the matter of the salvation of all the foreknown and fore-ordained is presented as an accomplished fact: they are justified, and called, and glorified. In the counsel of God He knows His own as saved and glorified sinners. And so, He blesses us with all spiritual blessings in heavenly places in Christ, "according as He hath chosen us in Him before the foundation of the world." Eph. 1:3, 4. "For

the children being not yet born, neither having done any
good or evil, that the purpose of God according to election
might stand, not of works, but of him that calleth; It
was said unto her, The elder shall serve the younger. As
it is written, Jacob have I loved, but Esau have I hated."
Rom. 9:11-13. And "it is not of him that willeth, nor of
him that runneth, but of God that sheweth mercy." Rom.
9:16. Yea, He hath "mercy on whom he will have mercy,
and whom he will he hardeneth." Rom. 9:18. O, indeed,
"whosoever will may come;" but this is also true: "no
man can come unto me, except the Father which hath
sent me draw him: and I will raise him up at the last
day." And again: "Therefore I said unto you, that no
man can come unto me, except it were given him of my
Father." John 6:44, 65. And have ye never read that
"except a man be born again he cannot see the kingdom
the God." And how shall a man seek that which he does
not even see?

It is plain, then, that when a man sings or preaches
"Whosoever will may come," he presents in song or sermon
what is undoubtedly true. And to this we have no objection. Indeed, it is true that whoever will may come to
Christ, and will surely be received. Never a man will
appear in the day of the revelation of the righteous judgment of God who will be able to say that he longed, and
desired, and willed, and sought earnestly to come, but
was refused. But if a man sings or preaches no more than
this, he, nevertheless, fails to present the full truth of
the gospel as it is in Christ Jesus and revealed to us in
Holy writ. He speaks a half truth which, because of
its deceptive nature, is more dangerous than a direct
and plain falsehood. A large part, the more basic and,
therefore, more important part of the truth he forgets

or intentionally omits. One may, indeed, freely proclaim "over vale and hill" that "whosoever will may come," but he is unfaithful to his ministry unless he adds: "no one can come unless the Father draw him;" it is not of him that willeth, nor of him that runneth, but of God that sheweth mercy."

This onesided emphasis on what man may do and must do in order to be saved without mention of the truth that the sinner can do nothing unless God first performs the wonder of His grace upon him, is characterictic of most collections of hymns in distinction from the beautiful and mighty Psalms. And this onesided presentation of the matter of salvation also predominates in modern, so-called evangelical preaching. And so the way is prepared for that caricature of gospel preaching, that consists chiefly in begging the sinner to come to Jesus before it is too late, leaves the false impression with him that it is quite in his power to come today or tomorrow, or whatever time may be convenient to him, and that presents a very willing but powerless Jesus, that would be ever so pleased to save the sinner, but is incapable to do so unless the sinner gives his consent. The "whosoever will may come" is presented as meaning: "All men can will to come whenever they please." And instead of the truth of the gospel that no man can come to Christ unless the Father draw him, we now hear; "No Christ can come to the sinner, except the sinner permit him!" Here is a fair example of it: "God is ready, God is willing, God is eager, God is anxious, God is pleading for the privilege of washing away the sins of every soul in the precious blood of His Son and heir. But his hands are tied, His power is limited, His grace is constrained by you. If you want to be saved, God is willing to save you. If you don't want to be saved, there isn't anything that even God can do to rescue you from that pit of eternal burning." That is what becomes of the preaching of the gospel when the truth of God's sovereign grace is either forgotten or denied. Call it the gospel, if you like; to me it is nothing short of blasphemy of the name of the living God! An anxious and pleading God, whose power is limited, and whose hands may be tied by the proud and stubborn sinner, who is less than dust of the balance, is no God, but a miserable idol!

And, therefore, I repeat: "Send the proclamation over vale and hill: whosoever will may come," provided you proclaim it, not as the whole gospel, but as only part of it, and that you do not fail to emphasize the other part: "It is not of him that willeth, nor of him that runneth, but of God that sheweth mercy." God is God. And He is the Lord, also in the matter of the salvation of the sinner. How these two, the sovereign will and grace of God, and the sinner's will to come, are related we hope to expound in future talks on this subject. Several questions are involved in this subject that must be answered. Whosoever will may come to whom, or to what? And for what purpose, to seek what, or to receive what, do they come? What does it mean to come? And how is it possible for the sinner to come?

But even now we must indicate in a general way what is the relation between the sovereign will of God to save, and the will of man to come. That this relation is not such, that the will of God depends on the will of man, so that the will of God is impotent to save unless man's will consents to be saved, is evident from all Scripture, and clearly follows from the simple but very fundamental truth that God is the Lord. Nor is the relation one of mere cooperation, as if man were a party in relation to God, and the will of man and of God meet and work together in the matter of the sinner's salvation. God is GOD! Over against Him man is never a party. To speak of cooperation between God and man, is like speaking of cooperation between the potter and his clay in the formation of a vessel. But that revelation is such that God's merciful and gracious will of salvation is ever first, mighty, irresistible, efficacious, operating upon the will of the sinner in such a way that he desires and longs and determines to come. The will to come on the part of the sinner is the fruit of the saving grace of God working in him mightily unto salvation. No one can come unto Christ unless the Father draw him!

And thus, he that will come may be quite sure that he may come, and that he will surely be received. Christ will not cast him out. His will to come is a sure manifestation of God's eternal purpose of salvation concerning him, and of the drawing power of His grace. Do you will to come to Christ? Is it your desire to come to Him as the Fount of living water, that you may drink? Do you long to come to Him as the Bread of life that you may eat? Do not hesitate, then! Do not stand afar off, discovering a thousand reasons in yourselves, why you could not possibly be received. For "whosoever will" may surely come and take of the water of life freely, because "whosoever will" is already drawn by the Father! You may hear the word of Christ: "All that the Father giveth me, shall come to me; and him that cometh unto me I will in no wise cast out!"

Coming to the God of Our Salvation

II

Coming to the God of Our Salvation

Incline your ear, and come unto me.
—Isa. 55:3.

WE are discussing the theme: "Whosoever will may come." And before we proceed, it may be expedient to consider these words from the well-known hymn somewhat more closely than we did thus far. We said that they were biblical provided they were properly interpreted, and given a biblical sense. We must bear in mind that they are nowhere literally found in Scripture. The text to which they most probably refer, Rev. 22:17, reads: "And let him that is athirst come. And whosoever will, let him take of the water of life freely." And the apparently slight alteration of these words in those of the hymn may lead to serious misunderstanding and error.

What is meant by "whosoever will may come?" The plain implication of these words is, evidently, that whosoever will is permitted, has the right to come, and need not be afraid that he will be refused. And to this we wholeheartedly agree. No one ever seeks without finding; no one ever asks without receiving; no one ever knocks in vain. No one that will come to Jesus shall ever find the way barred: he will surely be received. But the further question must be asked: why is this true? How do you explain that whosoever will has the right to come, and that he may be assured that he will not be cast out?

The answer that many give to this question, and that expresses most likely the meaning attached to the words of the hymn by the majority of those that sing it, runs somewhat as follows. All men have the right to come, if they will only take it, and insist upon their rights. Christ died for all men as far as God's intention is concerned, and, therefore, he obtained the right of salvation, the right to come to Him, for all. Moreover, all men have the power of will to come to Christ, if they will only use it aright. It is in their power either to accept or to reject Jesus. This it is that must be proclaimed to them. Men must be told that they have the right and the power to come to Christ, and the preaching by men must persuade them to make the right choice. Christ did all He could. And now He stands at the door of men's hearts and knocks, and He pleads and begs that the sinner will let Him in. But the key is on the inside. He cannot come into men's hearts unless they let Him. Salvation is for all, but it is up to man to take it. Whosoever will may come!

This interpretation of the words of the hymn is a serious error, as I hope to make plain. Serious the error is, because with a Christ that merited salvation for all men, but who cannot actually save the sinner unless the latter permits Him, salvation is utterly impossible. And over against this false doctrine we maintain that the saving grace of God, changing the heart of the sinner, precedes the will to come to Christ. The latter is the fruit of the former. Only where the irresistible and efficacious grace of God changes and radically turns about the perverse will of the sinner can the latter will to come to Christ. And no man has this will of himself. We must, therefore, investigate what is implied in the will to come. And in order to do so, we must first of all ask the question: to whom must the sinner come?

Perhaps, you will say: the answer to this question is quite simple. It is that we must come to Jesus. And this is quite true. But it is by no means a superfluous question: and who is this Jesus to Whom we must come? According to the impression that is left by many a preacher in our day, Jesus ought to be the most popular man in the world. He is someone who offers to save you from death and the eternal tortures of hell, and who will take you to a beautiful heaven after you die. It pays to come to Him. He is a wonderful paymaster, who pays the highest wages in the world. Besides, He leaves it entirely up to you, whether you will accept Him or not. It is in your power to do either. And you can make your choice any time, if only you do so before you die. Now, what could be more appealing to man than such a Jesus? And what could be more flattering to the sinner's pride than a Christ that is entirely in his power to accept or to reject? Surely, he must feel that he does Christ a great favor when he accepts Him, that he is a pretty good man to let Jesus in his heart, much better than others who reject Him, and that He makes a profitable bargain when he exchanges the services of the devil for that of this wonderful paymaster! And if he is only consistent, he ought to say in his prayers: "O God, what a good thing it was that I am not as other men, and that I was good enough to make it possible for Thee, and for Thy Christ, to save me!"

But on the very surface of things, it would seem plain that there is something fundamentally wrong with this presentation of Jesus. For, as far as mere men, natural

men, are concerned, there never was a more unpopular
man in all the world than the Christ of the Scriptures.
From the time that Cain murdered Abel till the present
day, all the world as "world" always hated Him. It was
for His sake that, in the old dispensation, they killed the
prophets, and stoned them that were sent by God to preach
Him. And when He Himself tabernacled among us in
the days of His flesh, it required only three years of
public ministry to arouse the popular disgust and hatred
against Him to such a pitch, that they cast Him out as
the lowest criminal, and nailed Him to the cross. He
Himself declares that the world hates Him, that they will
hate His people, and that His Church is always only a
little flock. On the very face of things, therefore, it would
appear that there is something radically amiss with the
presentation of a Jesus that appeals to the natural man,
and whom all men have the power to accept.

What then? To whom must we come?

The ultimate answer to this question is this: we must
come to GOD!

This is the teaching of the Word of God. "Look unto
me, and be ye saved, all the ends of the earth, for I am
God, and there is none else. I have sworn by myself,
the word is gone out of my mouth in righteousness, and
shall not return, That unto me every knee shall bow,
every tongue shall swear. Surely shall one say, in the
Lord have I righteousness and strength: even to him shall
all men come; and all that are incensed against him shall
be ashamed." Isa. 46:22-24. "Incline your ear, and come
unto me; hear, and your soul shall live. Isa. 55:3. "Let
the wicked forsake his way, and the unrighteous man his
thoughts: and let him return unto the Lord, and he will
have mercy upon him; and to our God, for he will abun-

dantly pardon. Isa. 55:7. "O Israel, return unto the Lord, thy God; for thou hast fallen by thine iniquity. Take with you words, and turn unto the Lord: and say unto him, Take away all iniquity, and receive us graciously; so will we render the calves of our lips.' Hos. 14:1, 2. "Therefore, also now, saith the Lord, turn ye even unto me with all your heart, and with fasting, and with weeping, and with mourning." Joel 2:12. "Seek ye me, and ye shall live," and again, "Seek the Lord, and ye shall live." Amos 5:4, 6. The Lord Jesus teaches us, that He is the way to the Father's house, and that no one cometh unto the Father, but by Him. John 14:6. And Christ is able to save them to the uttermost, that come unto God by him. Heb. 7:25.

O, indeed, we must come to God. "Whosoever will may come," means "whosoever will come to GOD may come to Him." We must come to God, not merely in order to obtain salvation, but to come to Him *is* salvation. It is not merely a means to an end, it is the end itself. We must come to God who is GOD, that is, not to a god of our own imagination, which is always an idol, but to the true and living God, as He reveals Himself to us in His Word. To God we must come, Who dwelleth in the light that no man can approach unto; Who is a light, and there is no darkness in Him at all; Who is good, that is, the fulness of all infinite perfections, righteousness, holiness, truth, and grace, and in Whose presence there is fulness of joy, pleasures forevermore! To God we must come, Who is too pure of eyes to behold iniquity, Who loveth the righteous, but Who is angry with the wicked every day, and Who is a consuming fire, the great, the glorious, the terrible God! We must come to Him, that is, we must enter into His blessed fellowship, into the

secrets of His friendship, into His most intimate communion, so that we dwell in His house as friends with their
Friend, taste that He is good, (know Him as we are known,
see Him face to face, walk with Him and talk with Him,
love Him as we are loved, have our delight in His will,
and glorify His name for evermore. O, yes, to be saved
is to be delivered from hell, provided you understand
that the torture of hell is exactly that there one feels the
wrath of God, and his being utterly forsaken by Him!
To be saved, to be sure, is to go to heaven, and heaven is
a beautiful place, a glorious house with many mansions,
a new creation, and a new Jerusalem, with streets of gold
and pearly gates, provided you understand that the heart
of it all, and the very essence of it all is that God is
there, the Father, and that there we shall forever walk
in the light of the glory of God that fills the city! For
to know God is life eternal. John 17:3. To come to
God,—that is our salvation! For:

> "To live apart from God is death;
> 'Tis good His face to seek."

And this stands to reason.

Man was originally so created that this true knowledge
of and perfect fellowship with the ever living God is his
very life, and that apart from this blessed fellowship
there is no life, but only death and hell for him. In his
very being he was so constituted that his nature was
adapted to bear the image of God, to be, in a creaturely
sense and measure, like God. And not only so, but with
the likeness of God he was endowed. After the image
of God, in true knowledge of God, in perfect righteousness,
in spotless holiness, he was created. And thus he was

capable of knowing God, of dwelling in His blessed fellow-ship of friendship, of loving Him and being loved, and of serving Him in freedom with all his heart and mind and soul and strength. That was man's life and bliss.

But man did not regard his bliss. He departed from the living God. He disregarded His Word, to heed the word of the devil. He violated God's covenant and trans-gressed His commandment. He proposed to seek his life and bliss far from the living God. And he became guilty, the object of God's just wrath, damnable and liable to death. The death sentence was executed upon him. He became darkness, corrupt in heart and mind, a slave of sin and of the devil, an enemy of God. That is man's misery. And, therefore, to God, to the living God, he must return, and to come again to Him is his salvation. "Whosoever will may come," indeed, provided you under-stand that this means nothing less than to come to the living God!

But how shall we come to God? We may not come to Him, for we are guilty because of our sins, we can only increase our guilt daily, and we have lost every right to dwell in the Father's house. We are exiles from the home of Father, neither have we the right to return. We dare not come to God, for He is holy and righteous, and He is terribly displeased with sin and with the workers of iniquity. How dare we come to Him, Who is a con-suming fire? We cannot come to God, for we are corrupt by nature, and the natural man is enmity against God. With God is the eternal light, and we love the darkness rather than the light. And because of our foolishness and hatred of God, we will not come to Him, but seek our happiness far from Him in the way of iniquity. How then, shall we come to the living God and be saved?

The answer to this question is: God has revealed Himself as the God of salvation through Jesus Christ our Lord! Hence, the answer to the question: to whom must we come? has not changed; it still is: we must come to God, to the living God; but it has assumed a new form: we must come to God through Jesus Christ, for He is able to save to the uttermost those that come to God by Him! To Jesus we must come, in order to come to God! For Jesus is the revelation of the God of our salvation!

And let it be emphasized that it is to Jesus Christ of the Scriptures that we must come, and not to any Christ of our own imagination. Many, indeed, are the modern Jesuses, all of whom are characterized by this that in order to come to them the sinner does not have to renounce the pride of his sinful heart. He is the great Teacher, whose instruction we are good enough to receive, especially as it is embodied in the Sermon on the Mount, and whose precepts we must keep. Or He is the good example, who Himself walked in the light, that we might follow in His steps. And so, we must ever walk and live with the question before our minds: what would Jesus do? Or He is the one who was deeply God-conscious, who was conscious of the truth that man is the son of God, and who revealed to us, that we, too, are sons of God. We must, therefore, believe in the Fatherhood of God, and establish the brotherhood of man in the world. We must build Christian character. We must establish the kingdom of God on earth. Jesus has shown us how good we really are, and what a power for good we have, and we can work ourselves into the favor and love of God All this modern trash that flatters the pride of sinful men has nothing to do with the Christ of the Scriptures.

We must come to Jesus. And Jesus leaves us nothing but the confession that we are sinners, damnable and

COMING TO THE GOD OF OUR SALVATION 31

corrupt, as far as we are concerned, sinners that must be and only can be saved by pure and sovereign grace. The Christ of the Scriptures is He that came into the world, the Son of God, the second Person of the Holy Trinity, as a helpless Babe in the manger of Bethlehem, flesh of our flesh, bone of our bone, from the virgin Mary. He is the One that tabernacled among us, and by His Word and work revealed unto us the Father, the God of our salvation. The Christ of the Scriptures is He that died on the cross of Calvary, not for His principle, not as a noble example for us to follow, but because He was delivered for our transgressions, and in our stead brought to God the perfect sacrifice for sins, fully satisfying the justice of God with respect to all our transgressions. He is the One that was raised on the third day because of our justification, raised to glorious, transcendent, victorious life; death hath no more dominion over Him. He is the Christ that ascended up on high, was exalted at the right hand of God, received all power in heaven and on earth, and received the promise of the Spirit. He is the quickening Spirit, the Saviour, the mighty Lord, who has the prerogative and the power to save sinners, that is, to bring them back to the living God, to lead them into Father's house, that they may have life, and have it more abundantly than ever before! In Him we behold the Reconciler, the Justifier of the ungodly, Who does not impute transgressions unto us. He is the Bread of life, which we must eat; the Fount of living water, from which we must drink. He is the way to the Father, and to come to Him is to come unto God by Him!

But who wants to come to God?

Does the natural man, of whom the Scriptures say that he is dead in trespasses and sins, Eph. 1:2; that he is darkness, that he loves darkness rather than light, and that he hates the light, neither cometh to the light, Eph. 5:8; John 3:19, 20; that he does not seek after God, that there is no fear of God before his eyes, and that his mind is emity against God, Rom. 3:11, 18; 8:7;—does that man, I say, have the will to come to God by Jesus Christ? To ask this question is to answer it: he will never come to the living God of himself.

But all the more sure it is that "whosoever will may come." For he that thirsts after the living God, has already been drawn by the Father. And if anyone will come to God through Christ, his mind has already been enlightened, and his will has been marvelously changed by the almighty grace of God, who called the things that are not as if they were, and who quickens the dead. Let him not doubt that he will be received, for Christ Himself assures him: "All that the Father giveth me, shall come to me; and him that cometh to me, I will in no wise cast out!"

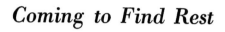

Coming to Find Rest

III

Coming to Find Rest

Come unto me, all ye that labor and are heavy laden, and I will give you rest. —MATT. 28:11.

IN order to be saved, we must come to God. And since we as sinners cannot possibly come to God as we are, guilty and defiled with sin, we must come to Jesus, in order that through Him we may come to God. For Jesus is the revelation of the God of our salvation, and He is able to save to the uttermost them that come unto God through Him. And all that will to come unto Him may surely come, and have the assurance that they shall not be cast out.

But who are they that will come to Jesus, to the Christ of the Scriptures? In whatever way you may explain the fact, it is evident that not all men have the desire and the will to come, for if they did, they would surely come to Him. Scripture and actual experience teach us plainly, however, that all men are not saved. And when the gospel is preached to men promiscuously, it soon becomes evident that many reject Him, must have none of Him, hate Him, and crucify Him afresh, while others receive Him and receive power to become the sons of God. Christ is set for a fall and rising again of many, and that not only in Israel, but throughout the ages of the present dispensation, and among all nations. Lu. 2.34.

He is a sign that is contradicted, and the thoughts of
many hearts are revealed through Him. Lu. 2:34, 35.
The word of the cross is foolishness to some, and a power
of God unto salvation for others. I Cor. 1:18. Christ
crucified is to many a stumbling block, while to thousands
He is the wisdom of God. I Cor. 1:23, 24. And those
that preach the gospel are a savor of life unto life to some,
but they are also, a savor of death unto death to many.
II Cor. 2:15, 16. He is the chief corner stone, elect,
precious, upon which many are built into a spiritual house,
an holy priesthood, to offer up spiritual sacrifices, acceptable
to God by Jesus Christ; but to others He is the stone
of stumbling and the rock of offense. I Pet. 2:5-7. Thus
it was when Jesus Himself was on earth, and preached
the gospel of the kingdom, and the same distinction and
separation between men is always caused by the gospel
of Christ.

The question arises: how do you explain this difference?
On the one hand we may ask: what is there about this
Jesus, this Christ of the Scriptures, that some should hold
Him above all things, and count all things but dross and
dung in comparison with the knowledge of Jesus their
Lord, while others despise and reject Him, and even hate
Him above all there is to be hated? And on the other
hand, the question is: what is there in men that they
should reveal such radically different evaluations of, and
assume such sharply opposing attitudes with respect to
the same Christ? Whosoever will may come, to be sure.
But all men do not will to come. Why not? And why
do some will to come to Him at all?

In order to find the answer to these questions we must
take a little closer look at the Christ of the Scriptures,
as well as at men in relation to Him. Who is this Jesus?

What does He claim to be? What does He promise to those that come to Him, and what must men seek, desire, love, in order to have the will to come? Especially those passages in which the Lord calls men to come unto Him demand our attention. And one of these is the well known passage from Matt. 11:28: "Come unto me, all ye that labor and are heavy laden, and I will give you rest.'

It is evident at once that the Saviour here presents Himself as the Rest-giver. And let us note at once that this statement is both positive and unlimited as to time and place. It is positive in its promise: I will give you rest. And it is precisely by such statements as these that the Saviour distinguished Himself from all that ever spoke. He spoke with authority, and not as the scribes. He does not say: I will instruct you in the art of securing rest for yourselves, or I will show you where you may find rest; but positively He declares: I will give you rest. And it is not limited to time or place, for He still speaks these words. More than nineteen hundred years ago He spoke them in the little country of Canaan. But He has spoken them ever since, and still speaks them, and that, too, in all the world. And still it is the only voice of power and authority that is heard in the midst of a world full of unrest, war, hatred, bloodshed, and destruction: Come unto me, and I will give you rest!

We may, probably, be inclined to think, that all the world, especially the war-torn and war-weary world of today, would heed this voice, and turn to Him for rest. O, it is true, we are at war. We are fighting the bitterest, the deadliest, the most destructive war that was ever fought. But are we not fighting for peace, for universal rest to succeed this terrible struggle? Are we not seriously seeking, talking about, planning a real, a just, a durable peace for the whole world? Well, then, the solution seems simple. Here is the voice of authority, causing itself to be heard to the utmost ends of the world: Come unto Me, I will give you rest! Surely, all men will come to Him, that He may realize His promise to them!

But what is this rest He promises?

Frequently Scripture speaks of rest, and the idea of it is always essentially the same. In six days God created the world, and on the seventh day He rested. That was God's rest, His Sabbath, His entering into the enjoyment of His finished work. And He sanctified that day for man, that he, too, might enter into the rest of God. The land of Canan, into which Jehovah led His people Israel, was the rest: there the people were to dwell in covenant-fellowship with the Lord their God. And He commanded them to keep the sabbath, the rest of the Lord. But the people that do err in their hearts, and that do not know His ways, are the objects of His wrath to whom He swears that they shall never enter into His rest. Ps. 95:10, 11. In the way of Jehovah's precepts the people shall find rest for their souls. Jer. 6:16. The first part of the fourth chapter of the epistle to the Hebrews is entirely devoted to the discussion of this rest. And there we learn, that neither the rest of creation in the first paradise, nor the rest of the land of Canaan, was final and perfect: God had planned another, a better, a richer and more enduring rest for His people, the rest in Christ, the eternal Sabbath that remains for the people of God. And now we must labor to enter into that rest. Heb. 4:1-11. And of that rest speaks the voice from heaven in Rev. 14:13: "Blessed are the dead which die in the Lord from henceforth: Yea, saith the Spirit, that they may rest from their labors; and their works do follow them." It is the very opposite of the state of the wicked, that worship the beast and his image, the smoke of whose torment "ascendeth up for ever and ever, and they have no rest day or night." Rev. 14:11. From beginning to end the Scriptures speak of this rest as the realization of the promise of God to His people. And it is of this same rest that the Saviour speaks when He calls: Come unto Me, and rest!

What, then, is rest in general, and what is this particular rest that is held before us in the Scriptures as the final goal of salvation?

Rest is not the same as idleness or mere inactivity. For, on the one hand, it is quite possible to stretch one's limbs on the bed of indolence without finding rest, and a state of strict inactivity is impossible for man: his spirit is ever busy. And, on the other hand, a state of full and highest activity is quite compatible with perfect rest. God is pure activity, yet He is always in the state of perfect rest. In that beautiful and highly symbolic picture of the state of glory presented in Rev. 4, we read of the four living creatures that stand around the throne of God and of the Lamb that "they rest not day and night, saying, Holy, holy, holy, Lord God Almighty, which was, and is, and is to come." vs. 8. Yet, who does not understand that in this incessant glorification of the Most High they enjoy the perfect rest? Even the rest of our weekly sabbath does not consist in mere cessation from all work, but rather in filling the day to capacity with the activity of seeking the kingdom of God. And a man that loafs his time away on the first day of the week, may be a worse desecrater of the sabbath than he that spends the whole day in the shop or on his farm.

Rest implies that a certain task is finished, that the work is accomplished and perfected, that the purpose has been attained and the goal is reached, and that now we enter into the enjoyment of the finished work. It is the state of soul and body, of mind and heart in which the highest activity is at the same time perfect repose, and work is perfect joy.

For man, this rest is the perfect fellowship with the living God. The famous saying of Augustine is quite true: "Our heart is restless, until it rests in Thee." For man was made after the image of God, in true righteousness and holiness, endowed with the knowledge of God which is life, in order that in this likeness of God he might be God's friend, enter into His most secret communion, enjoy His favor and taste that the Lord is good. And in this fellowship he was to be constantly active, love the Lord His God with all his heart and mind and soul and strength, and serve the Most High with his whole being in willing obedience. In that state of perfect rest and highest activity, of joy and peace, of life and bliss, in which he constantly reached the goal of fellowship with God in the way of perfect obedience of love, God placed man in the state of rectitude in the first paradise. And of this perfect relation of labor and rest the weekly cycle of six days and one was to be symbol and seal to him.

But man fell out of the rest of God into the hopeless unrest of the devil. He disregarded the Word of his God, and turned to follow the lie of the serpent. He sinned. He refused to walk in that way of obedience in which alone the rest of God's blessed fellowship could be attained and tasted. And he became an exile from God's house, guilty and worthy of death, an object of the wrath of God under which he pines and dies, darkened in his understanding, corrupt in heart and perverse of will, an enemy of God, seeking rest where only unrest can be found, peace where there is only war, life in death. He bears a load of guilt for which he can never atone, but which he can only increase daily; he is chained with shackles of sin and corruption which he is not able to break; and he is in the power of death which he is incapable to overcome. Restlessly he wanders, without God in the world, and he "is like the troubled sea, when it cannot rest, whose waters cast up mire and dirt. There is no peace, saith my God, to the wicked." Isa. 57:20, 21.

God, however, had provided a better rest for His people, the rest of His eternal kingdom and covenant, in which His tabernacle would be with men forever, and that, too, in heavenly glory. And the work of God, whereby He lifts us out of the depth of our unrest into the glory of the eternal sabbath, His rest, is the wonder of grace and salvation. For also this final and eternal rest can be attained only in the way of perfect obedience ,and this time in the way of an obedience that is sufficient to blot out and overcome sin. The justice of God must be satisfied, sin must be atoned, a basis of righteousness must be established. And the sinner must be redeemed, and liberated from the power and dominion of sin and death, and clothed with a new righteousness, endowed with a new life, in order that he may have the right, and the power to eat of the tree of life which is in the midst of the paradise of God. Rest, therefore, is cessation from sin, the state in which the power of sin and death has been vanquished forever, and the goal of perfect righteousness and eternal life in God's heavenly tabernacle has been reached.

That rest is in Christ. We could never accomplish the task of atoning for our sins, nor could we ever deliver ourselves from the bondage of corruption and the dominion of death. Heavy laden are we, and even if we would toil to atone for our sins, we would but labor in vain. The work is God's. The rest is His. He accomplished the work in and through Christ, His only begotten Son. Christ is the rest in His very Person, for He is Immanuel, God with us; the divine and human nature are forever united in His blessed Person. He merited the rest, for He took all our sins upon His mighty shoulders, and bore the whole burden of them upon the accursed tree. He accomplished the task, for he cried out: "It is finished." He took all our guilt away, overcame the power of death, and issued forth into the glory of His resurrection-life. And He went into the highest heavens, and received the promise of the Spirit, so that He is the quickening Spirit, able to deliver us from sin unto righteousness, from death into eternal life. And from there He calls: "Come unto Me, all ye that labor, and are heavy laden, and I will give you rest."

But will men come unto Him? Have they the desire and the will to enter into His rest? Not, to be sure, of themselves! For the will to come is motivated by the longing to return to God, and man is an enemy of God. The will to come implies the consciousness and the acknowledgement of our being heavy laden, laden with a burden of sin, which we can never remove. It implies that we know that we are weary, weary of sin and death, and that we toil in vain. It means that we have come to the acknowledgment that, as far as we are concerned, the task is impossible: there is no way out, no way into the rest. It means that we have eyes to see Jesus as the Restgiver, and that we long for Him, that He may bring us to God, and into rest. We want to get right with God, and we know not how; we want to cease from sin, and we cannot; we want to go home, and we may not. But Christ knows,

and He is able, and in Him is our hope. Such is the will
to come.

But the natural man of himself has not this will. He is
weary, to be sure, but not of sin. He is weary of unrest,
of war, of destruction, of bloodshed, of sickness, of sorrow,
of death. And he labors and toils to improve his condition,
to establish peace and happiness, to make a better world.
But he does not acknowledge that his burden is his sin,
and that all his unrest finds its cause in the fact that he
has forsaken God. He does not want to cease from sin.
He does not seek after God. He seeks rest in the sphere
of sin. Speaking beautiful words of peace, he makes war,
boasting of righteousness he hates the righteousness of
God, claiming to labor for a better world, he destroys it.
And he does not will to enter into the rest of God, and to
come to Christ.

But Christ speaks: Come! And when *He* speaks, who
can still resist? Ah, when I speak, when mere man speaks,
when a preacher begs and calls and persuades, it is of no
avail. You hear with the natural ear, you see with your
natural eye, you understand the meaning of the gospel,
but you refuse to come, you reject the Christ, you only
prove that you are blind, and deaf, and very corrupt, and
aggravate your guilt. But Christ speaks! He that once
stood at the open grave of Lazarus, calling: "Lazarus, come
forth," and he came out, speaks. He speaks by his Spirit
and Word. And through the power of His almighty Word
you receive eyes to see, ears to hear, an enlightened understanding to know your misery, the longing to be delivered
and to enter into the rest of God, the will to come to
Christ! And whosoever will may come! The promise is
yours, and it shall never fail: "Come, and I will give you
rest!"

Coming to Drink

IV

Coming to Drink

If any man thirsts, let him come unto
me and drink.   —JOHN 7:37.

MOST generally, the words of the well-known hymn:
"whosoever will may come," are interpreted as meaning that salvation is a matter that is left up to the will and
choice of the sinner. It is true, all men are not saved, for
all men do not will to come to Christ. But that they do
not will is not due to any incapacity of the will and
spiritual darkness of the understanding, but simply to a
wrong use of their willpower. Man is master of his own
will. Even though it may be granted that by nature he
is inclined to reject salvation and Christ, he has the power
to turn about and accept Him. He can will as he pleases,
and please as he wills. The will of man is free, sovereignly
free, arbitrarily free. Man can will to accept Christ, and
he can will to reject Him. And this situation prevails
until he dies. Even as he is able to accept Christ to-day,
so he may reject Him again, and apostatize from the faith,
tomorrow. He may come to the Saviour to-day, and forsake Him tomorrow. If only he accepts Him just before
he dies, or is faithful to Him till that moment, he is saved.
But if he should accept Him all his life, and reject Him
at the last moment, he is lost. Nor is it from this view-
point quite clear, why if this arbitrariness is essential to free-

47

dom of the will, the saints in glory are not continually in danger of rejecting Christ, and plunging from glory into desolation.

This view we reject. Not only is it contrary to all that the Scriptures teach us concerning the state of the natural man, and concerning the sovereign grace of God to save, but it is also absurd, and contrary to actual experience. An arbitrary will of man, that can turn either this way or that, that can arbitrarily will either one thing or its opposite, simply does not exist. The will is motivated in its choice. This is true in respect to natural things. Why do you will to eat? Because you are hungry. Why do you drink? Because you are thirsty. You cannot will to eat when you are full and nauseated. But the same is true spiritually. Also the will to come to Christ is motivated. Why does man come to Christ? Because he longs after the living God. Because he is weary of sin, and seeks rest, the rest of forgiveness, of eternal righteousness, of fellowship with the God of his salvation, and because he acknowledges that it is only in and through Christ that he can attain to them. Why does a man come to Christ? Because he thirsts for the living water, and the Fount of that water of life is opened in Christ alone. And this longing after God, after forgiveness and righteousness, this thirst for the water of life, this will to come to Christ, is not of the sinner himself: it is the fruit of grace.

Christ is the Fount of the water of life. The river of the water of life in the paradise of God flows from the throne of God and of the Lamb, which means that it proceeds from God through Christ. In the last day, the great day of the feast of the tabernacles, when the golden pitcher was filled with water from the pool of Siloam, Jesus stood and cried: "If any man thirsts, let him come unto me and

drink." John 7:37. To the Samaritan woman at the well
the Lord says: "If thou knewest the gift of God, and
who it is that saith to thee, Give me to drink; thou wouldst
have asked of him, and he would have given thee living
water." And again: "Whosoever drinketh of this water
shall thirst again: but whosoever drinketh of the water that
I shall give him shall never thirst; but the water that I
shall give him shall be in him a well of living water.' John
4:10, 13, 14. The opening of this fountain of living water
in Christ was typified and foretold ages before in the old
dispensation. The thirst of the children of Israel was wonderfully quenched with water out of the rock, and the
apostle Paul referring to this miracle of grace writes, that
they all drank "the same spiritual drink: for they drank
of that spiritual Rock that followed them: and that Rock
was Christ." I Cor. 10:4. Christ followed them all through
their wanderings in the desert, and revealed Himself by
supplying them with water from the rocks. With a view
to His coming Isaiah called: "Ho, every one that thirsteth,
come ye to the waters, and he that hath no money; come
ye, buy and eat; yea, come, buy wine and milk without
money and without price." Isa. 55:1. And he could proclaim the blessed promise: "For I will pour water upon
him that is thirsty, and floods upon the dry ground." Isa.
44:3. Through his prophet Zechariah the Lord promised:
"In that day there shall be a fountain opened to the house
of David and to the inhabitants of Jerusalem for sin and for
uncleanness." And "living waters shall go out from Jerusalem" in that day of great salvation. Zech. 13:1; 14:8. That
fountain is opened in Christ, and from Him flow the streams
of living water.

Let us ask the question: what is the meaning of this
symbol?

Water has a rich symbolic meaning in Scripture. Sometimes it symbolizes deep affliction that overwhelms one's soul, and threatens to drown him and swallow him up. As a sign of spiritual realities, it signifies especially three things: separation, cleansing, and spiritual quickening and refreshment. The water of baptism is a sign and seal of spiritual separation from the world into the fellowship of Christ, and of cleansing from sin unto eternal righteousness. Thus the waters of the deluge were typical of baptism into Christ, for by the flood it was, not by the ark, that the church was cleansed and separated from the ungodly world that perished in the waters of the flood. I Pet. 3:20, 21. In the same way the waters of the Red Sea typified baptism, for by these the people of Israel were separated unto God from Pharaoh and his host, and the house of bondage in Egypt. And through baptism the old man of sin is swallowed up, the new man in Christ arises, separated from sin and from the evil world, and raised with Christ into a new life of fellowship with God.

It is evident, however, that when Christ is presented as the fount of the water of life, from which we must drink, the meaning of the symbol is somewhat different. It is not spiritual cleansing, but quickening, refreshment, complete satisfaction that is signified. It may be said, first of all, that living water or water of life represents principally, and in its deeper sense, the Holy Spirit, as the Spirit of Christ, by Whom all the spiritual blessings of salvation are bestowed upon the Church as a whole, and upon believers individually. He is this stream of living water that flows constantly out of God, through Christ into the Church. This is evident from Isa. 44:3, for after the prophet has said "I will pour water upon him that is thirsty," he explains the symbolism by adding "I

will pour my Spirit upon thy seed." Thus also in John
7:37-39. The promise of living water is explained by the
apostle in the words: "But this spake he of the Spirit
which they that believe on him should receive." And this
is also evident from the picture of the river of the water
of life in Rev. 22, for the river is presented as flowing
from the throne of God and the Lamb. With the exalta-
tion of the Saviour and the outpouring of the Holy Spirit
soon after, on the day of Pentecost, the promise was fulfilled, the river of the water of life began to flow, and the
fount of living water was opened.

But the stream of living water represents the Spirit
as the Author of our salvation, who realizes unto us and
within us all the spiritual blessings in heavenly places that
are in Christ, and which He obtained for us by His perfect
obedience. These blessings are in the exalted Christ, and
the Spirit of Christ takes them out of Him to bestow
them upon us. He is called the Spirit of life, the Spirit
of adoption whereby we cry, Abba, Father; the Spirit of
truth, that leads us into all the truth; the quickening
Spirit, the Spirit of wisdom and knowledge and revelation,
the Spirit of holiness and sanctification, the Spirit of Christ.
Accordingly, it is He that regenerates us, and causes up to be
born of God, making us partakers of the resurrection-
life of Christ. He gives us understanding and discernment
of spiritual things, eyes to see, and ears to hear, and hearts
to understand the mysteries of the kingdom of heaven. It
is by Him that we are called from darkness into light,
from sin unto righteousness, from corruption into holiness,
from death into life. All the spiritual blessings of knowledge
and wisdom, of life and glory, of righteousness and holiness,
and all other riches of grace constantly flow from Christ
in the Spirit into the Church and into the believers. By

these they live, and are constantly refreshed unto eternal
life. And this stream of spiritual blessings is symbolized
by the living water, or the river of the water of life.

All these spiritual blessings of salvation have their ground
and heart in one, namely, perfect righteousness. Righteousness and salvation are so closely and inseparably connected,
that Scripture sometimes virtually identifies them. Just
as the real essence of our misery is sin, so the heart of
our salvation is righteousness. Without righteousness there
is no life, no favor of God, no fellowship with Him. Righteousness is life and joy. We must, therefore, be made
righteous, and that, too, both in the legal and juridical
sense, and in the spiritual, ethical sense of the word. We
must be justified. Our sins must be blotted out and forgiven, and the perfect righteousness of God in Christ must
be imputed to us, so that, even though in ourselves we lie
in the midst of sin and death, we glory in our justification,
and are assured that we are righteous before God. But
we must also be sanctified, delivered from darkness and
corruption and all defilement, and quickened unto a new
life of holiness unto God. And in this comprehensive
sense of the word righteousness is our salvation. And,
therefore, it may finally be said that the water of life that
flows from the throne of God and the Lamb, is a stream of
constant righteousness, forgiveness, light, holiness, love of
God, eternal life! And blessed are they that hunger and
thirst after righteousness, for they shall be filled!

We must come, then, to Christ, in order to drink the
water of life, that is, to receive from Him, and to appropriate
unto ourselves all the spiritual blessings of grace, to obtain
righteousness and life. Christ calls: "come unto me, and
drink." Let us clearly understand this. The Christ of
the Scriptures, the Son of God in the flesh, Who dwelled

among us, Who revealed unto us the Father, and spoke the words of eternal life, Who was delivered unto the death of the cross for our transgressions, and was raised on the third day for our justification, Who was exalted in the highest heavens, and Who received the promise of the Holy Spirit, Who, finally, on the day of Pentecost poured out His Spirit into the Church,—that Christ is the open Fount of the water of life. He is our righteousness. He is our complete redemption. And He imparts Himself and all the blessings of salvation unto us through His Spirit. But this is done in such a way, that we receive and appropriate these blessings of salvation by a conscious and willing act on our part corresponding to Christ's act of imparting Himself to us. This act on our part is expressed by the words: "come and drink!" The water of life, if I may retain the figure for a moment, is not poured down our throat without any act on our part, or even against our will. Even if such a thing were possible, we would never taste its pure and refreshing sweetness. But it is the will of God that we taste it, for we are saved to the glory of His grace in the Beloved. He wills that we taste His grace, that we consciously experience the wonder of His grace. We must come and drink the water of life!

But what does it mean to come and drink from the Fountain of this living water? It implies that we are thirsty: "if any man thirsts, let him come unto me, and drink." "Ho, every one that is thirsty, come ye to the waters!" This thirst for the living water belongs to the will to come. Unless a sinner thirsts after the water of life, that is, principally after righteousness, he will never come to Christ, nor does he have the will to drink. And this means, first of all, that there is in his soul a profound consciousness of his sinful state, of his lost condition, of his being devoid of all righteousness, and of his being full of sin and corrup-

tion that make him damnable before God. It implies that
he deplores his sin in true repentance, that he longs for
forgiveness, and for the deliverance from the power and
the dominion of sin. He longs to be clothed with righteousness. It signifies, too, that he recognizes Christ as the
Fount of living water, as the fulness of righteousness and
life out of which he must drink and longs to drink. He
yearns for the full Christ and all the blessings of salvation.
He thirsts for the water of life. But this is not enough.
Thirsting he must hear and heed the word of Christ:
"Come unto me, and drink." He must not merely recognize
his own misery and the riches of the Saviour, but he must
now turn to Him, receive Him, believe on Him, and by
faith draw out of Him forgiveness and righteousness, wisdom
and knowledge, light and life eternal! Then he drinks
and his soul shall be satisfied.

"Ho, every one that thirsteth, come ye to the waters!"
"Come unto me, and drink! Let him that is athirst come!
And whosoever will, let him take of the water of life
freely!" To be sure, whosoever will may come to Christ
to drink of the living water!

But who will come? What is the relation between Christ
as the Fount of living water and the sinner? Is it thus,
that He is simply the overflowing Fountain of living water,
that He sends out preachers to call the attention of men
to this fountain, and that He now waits until they come,
and drink? Ah, but in that case no one would come. All
would despise the water of life! For all men are by nature
children of wrath, dead through trespasses and sins, and
they walk according to the course of this world, fulfilling
the desires of the flesh and of the mind. They thirst, yes,
but not after righteousness. They crave after the things
of this world, the lust of the flesh, the lust of the eyes,
the pride of life. And always the natural man boasts of

his own righteousness, and spurns the righteousness of God! And if it depends upon the will of that man, whether or not he will come to the Fountain of living water, and drink, he will never come. Nor will a veritable army of begging and hawking preachers persuade him to come. No man has of himself the will to come.

But the living Christ is first. And our will to come and take of the water of life freely is only the reaction of His own gracious act of imparting Himself to us. He imparts Himself to us, and we receive Him. He gives us spiritual eyes to see our own misery and spiritual wretchedness, and the riches of His fulness, and we behold Him as we never saw Him before. He draws us, and we come. He makes us thirsty and we drink. He changes our heart, and our mind, and our will by His Spirit and Word, and we find Him more precious than all the riches of the world, and consider all things but dung for the excellency of the knowledge of Christ Jesus our Lord.

Let no man, then, glory in himself!

For if you do not thirst for the living Christ, it is only because you are blind, and dead, and naked and miserable, an enemy of God, hating righteousness though boasting of your goodness, loving the darkness rather than the light, glorying in your shame. And boast not against the Christ of God, as if you had the power to decide to come to Him whenever you please. Christ is the Lord. No one can come to Him unless the Father draw him!

On the other hand, ye that thirst, and come unto Him to drink, exalt not yourselves. Ye came not of yourselves. It was His grace that made you thirst for the living water. It was He that called: Come! and you came. It was He that imparted Himself to you, and you drank, and continue to drink unto everlasting life! He that glorieth, let him glory in the Lord!

Coming to Eat the Bread of Life

V

Coming to Eat the Bread of Life

*For the bread of God is He which com-
eth down from heaven, and giveth life
unto the world.* —JOHN 6:33.

ONE of the most amazing miracles of the old dispensation is the feeding of the people of Israel, day by day,
with bread that rained from heaven, the wonderful manna.
How mysterious, how utterly inexplicable was this heavenly
bread! In appearance it was a little kernel, like coriander
seed, and as it fell with the early morning dew, it looked
like hoarfrost. Every morning it fell, and it never failed,
yet on the sabbath one looked for it in vain. It supplied
the children of Israel with bread only for one day, and if
they tried to lay up for the morrow, it became putrified
in their larders; yet, if on the sixth day they gathered
enough to last them over the sabbath, it was never spoiled.
Early in the morning it must be gathered, for the rising
sun would soon melt it; yet, it was so hard that it was
beaten and crushed with mortars, and it was baked in
the fire. It was meant only for the people of God, and
for none other, for it fell only around the camp of the
Israelites, and that, too, only as they wandered in the
desert: the like of it was never seen before, nor ever again.
To speak in terms of today, it must have been a very
healthful and palatable food, possessing all the necessary

vitamins, for it was capable of keeping over a million people alive and strong for a period of forty years! Indeed, the manna that rained from heaven was one of the most marvelous signs ever displayed!

Similarly, one of the most illustrious wonders performed by our Saviour during His public ministry among us, is the feeding of the five thousand at the shores of the Sea of Tiberias. Five loaves of bread and two small fishes were multiplied in His hands until there was sufficient food for five thousand hungry men, and the disciples could gather twelve basketfulls of the fragments that remained. Small wonder that the multitude were aroused to wild enthusiasm by the sight, and would take Him by force to crown Him their king! Of the manna in the desert they had heard through Moses, but this miracle surpassed even that in glory, for here they had but to sit down on the hillside to receive food prepared to eat!

Yet, these signs of God's marvellous power, taking place in the sphere of the natural and earthy, were but symbols obsignating still greater and more mysterious wonders of grace in the sphere of the spiritual and heavenly. For with reference to the wonder of the manna in the desert the apostle Paul writes in I Cor. 10:3 that the people of Israel "did all eat the same spiritual meat." And to the victorious saints the Lord promises that He will give them "to eat of the hidden manna." Rev. 2:17. And when on the day following the multiplication of the loaves He met those that had been fed in Capernaum, He rebuked them that they followed Him for the bread, and that they had not seen the sign. And He expounds to them the meaning of the sign by pointing to Himself as the bread of life. "For the bread of God is he which cometh down from heaven, and giveth life unto the world . . . I am the bread of life:

he that cometh to me shall never hunger . . . I am the bread which came down from heaven. . . He that believeth on me hath everlasting life.   I am that bread of life." John 6:33-48.

It is evident, then, that he that comes to Jesus must come to Him as the bread of life, and that the will to come and eat of that bread, implies and presupposes hunger, spiritual hunger. The dead do not eat. They that are full do not seek bread. One must have spiritual appetite to come to Jesus. In that sense it is true: "Whosoever will may come. We must, therefore, inquire what it means that Jesus is the bread of life, how one eats of this bread, and who have the will to come to eat.

In order to understand the meaning of the figurative expression "the bread of life," we must remember that "man doth not live by bread alone, but by every word that proceedeth out of the mouth of God." Deut. 8:3; Matt. 4:4, etc. And this does not mean, as it is often interpreted, that bread does not nourish us unless God blesses it, but that man is more than the beast, that he has a higher life, that cannot be sustained and nourished by mere material bread, but is dependent upon the Word of God's grace. The animal is purely earthy and physical. His life is sustained by bread alone. Man, however, is a creature that is adapted to a higher life, the spiritual life in fellowship with God. The saying, which appears to be the slogan of thousands in our mad, eminently carnal age, "let us eat, and drink, for tomorrow we die," is a denial of man's inmost nature and needs, and lowers him to the level of the brute beast. He has a higher life, which material bread, which all the things of this world, which all the products of culture and civilization cannot satisfy, but which can be satisfied and nourished only by the favor of God.

That this is, indeed, the meaning of the text we quoted is evident from its original context in Deut. 8:3, as well as from the use our Lord makes of it in reply to the first temptation of the devil. In Deut. 8:3 we read: "And he humbled thee, and suffered thee to hunger, and fed thee with manna, which thou knewest not, neither did thy fathers know; that he might make thee know that man doth not live by bread only, but by every word that proceedeth out of the mouth of the Lord doth man live." Manna was a sign of God's favor over His people, and in that sense it was "spiritual bread." I Cor. 10:3. And the Lord quotes this passage when the devil would tempt Him to reveal His power in making bread out of stones, to leave the way of suffering, and thus to become disobedient to the Father, which would cause Him to lose God's favor. He would much rather suffer hunger than lose the loving-kindness and fellowship of God, for man shall not live by bread alone, but by every word that proceedeth out of the mouth of God. For man it is true, indeed, what the psalmist so beautifully expresses in Ps. 63:

> "Apart from Thee I long and thirst,
> And nought can satisfy;
> I wander in a desert land
> Where all the streams are dry."

And again:

> "The lovingkindness of my God
> Is more than life to me;
> So will I bless Thee while I live
> And lift my prayers to Thee.
> In Thee my soul is satisfied,
> My darkness turns to light,
> And joyful meditations fill
> The watches of the night."

The reason for this is that man is more than the beast. He is a creature that is adapted to bear the image of God. He was formed by God's very fingers, and God breathed into his nostrils the breath of life. He was related to the earth, and to earthy things, to be sure, but also to God. He was formed with a *heart* whence are the issues of his life. And he was originally endowed with the image of God. He was gifted with the true knowledge of God, that he might know his Creator in love; he was created in perfect righteousness, that he might will the will of God; and he was made in spotless holiness, that he might consecrate himself and all things to the Most High. And thus, adorned with God's image, he lived. He thirsted after God, but his thirst was constantly satisfied. He knew his God in all things, lived in His fellowship, tasted His grace, and loved Him with all his heart, and with all his mind, and with all his soul, and with all his strength. The grace of God was the bread of life for him.

Such is man's real life.

All existence of man without this fellowship of God, apart from Him and under His wrath, is death. Man may eat and drink, he may work and enjoy himself with the things of this world, he may enhance his earthly existence with all the inventions of culture and art, but if he has no more than this he is very really dead.

And dead he is by nature, apart from Christ.

For he did not believe that he lived by the Word that proceeds out of the mouth of God. He rejected God's Word. He turned to the lie of the devil. In contradiction to the Word of God, he saw that the tree was good for food, and to make one wise. And he followed the lie. The result was that he died. He forfeited and lost the favor of God. He became the object of God's wrath, under which he pines and dies for ever. The image of God in him was perverted into its very opposite. Instead of his original knowledge of God, there now was darkness of mind, so that he loves and follows the lie and vanity; instead of righteousness, there were now the motions of iniquity, so that his will is perverse, and motivated by enmity against God; and instead of holiness, there is now the corruption of his whole nature, so that, rather than being consecrated to God, he lifts his rebellious fist in the face of the Almighty. He is become a child of his father the devil. Such is man by nature. And whoever denies this, and proclaims that all men are by nature the children of God, deceives the people, and leads them away from Christ. So dead man is, that by nature he does not and cannot hunger and thirst after the living God. So really dead is he, that he must be raised from the dead, that he must be born again, in order to live at all!

Now, Christ is the bread of life exactly for such sinners that are in themselves dead in trespasses and in sin. He is the Wonderbread of God, prepared by God in order that those that eat of it might have eternal life. And eternal life is not merely life that lasts for ever, but it is life in God's fellowship and friendship on the highest possible level, that is, in heavenly glory. Unto that everlasting life of immortality and incorruption in God's tabernacle, where we shall see face to face, and know as we are known, the God of our salvation nourishes us through Jesus Christ our Lord. He is the true manna that came down from heaven, the bread of life. He is such as the Son of God that became flesh, that was crucified, raised from the dead on the third day, glorified in the highest heavens, and is become the quickening Spirit. He is the bread of life for sinners because in Him there is fulness of grace, the grace which sinners need in order to have life. In Him there is righteousness, eternal righteousness, for sinners that are in themselves guilty, and worthy of eternal death, children of wrath; a righteousness that is sufficient to overcome and blot out all their sins, and to make them worthy of the glory of that eternal life which even Adam in the state of rectitude never knew, nor could have attained. In Him there is the power of complete liberation from the bondage and shackles of sin and corruption, the perfect liberty of the love of God. In Him there is perfect peace, knowledge of God, wisdom, light, and life. The Christ of the Scriptures is, indeed, the Bread of life, from which if a man eat, he shall never hunger. He is the true manna that is able to nourish the sinner from guilt unto perfect righteousness, from corruption unto holiness, from spiritual ignorance unto the true knowledge of God, from folly unto wisdom, from darkness unto light, from death unto eternal life!

In order to be saved, therefore, we must come to Him and eat. And as Christ does not simply *give* us, but *is* the bread of life, we must eat *Him*. Just as in the natural sense we eat bread, that is, take it, taste it, relish it, assimilate it, make it part and parcel of our very physical existence, flesh of our flesh, blood of our blood, bone of our bone; so, in the spiritual sense, we must eat the Christ of the Scriptures, appropriate Him, taste that He is good, absorb Him, and assimilate Him into our spiritual nature. We must eat Him, not as the modern Christ of man's own invention, not as the great teacher that instructs us how to be good, or as the good example we must copy, but as the crucified One Who was raised from the dead. That is the reason why Jesus said to the murmuring and astonished multitude in Capernaum: "And the bread that

I will give is my flesh, which I will give for the life of the world." And again: "Verily, verily, I say unto you, Except ye eat the flesh of the Son of man, and drink his blood, ye have no life in you. Whoso eateth my flesh, and drinketh my blood, hath eternal life; and I will raise him up at the last day. For my flesh is meat indeed, and my blood is drink indeed. He that eateth my flesh and drinketh my blood, dwelleth in me, and I in him." John 6:51-56. Thus appropriating and assimilating unto ourselves and into our spiritual substance the Christ of the Scriptures, we receive out of His fulness even grace for grace. His righteousness becomes our righteousness, His knowledge becomes our knowledge. His love overcomes our enmity, His life is victorious over our death: we are saved from death unto life.

Nor is this act of eating the bread of life ever an accomplished and finished deed. You cannot say: "I accepted Christ a year, or ten years ago, and because of that accomplished act I am saved and live to day." Even as for the sustenance of your physical existence you must continually eat bread, so you must constantly appropriate and assimilate Christ in order to have life. Always our life is in Him, never in us apart from Him; and always we must receive out of Him even grace for grace. And here in this world this eating of the bread of life takes place through the means of the preaching of the Word as revealed in the Scriptures, and through the administration of the holy sacraments which He Himself has instituted for that very purpose.

Whosoever will may come, and eat the bread of life! That is undoubtedly true. There is no exception to this "whosoever." But who will come? Who have this will to come? Surely, you will answer this question by saying: only those that hunger for the bread of life. The will to come is motivated by the hunger for this bread. And this hunger consists of a deep consciousness of one's own emptiness and of Christ's fulness, of one's own sin and of Christ's righteousness, of one's own death and of Christ's life; and of a profound longing and desire to possess Him!

But you will admit that the dead hunger not, and the natural man is dead, blind, naked, miserable, an enemy of God, a lover of sin and darkness. His condition is such that by nature he is not merely incapable of longing for the bread of life: it is nauseating to him, and he turns away from it in disgust. Always he will assume the same attitude as did the carnal multitude in Capernaum, when they finally judged that the Word of life Jesus spoke was a hard speech, which no one could hear, left Him, and walked no more with Him!

The will to come and eat of the bread of life is the will of faith. By faith only we hunger after righteousness and life. By faith only we recognize the Christ as the bread of life. By faith we long for Him, come to Him, are united with Him, draw out of Him even grace for grace, eat Him unto eternal life. But faith is not of ourselves. It is the gift of God. The will to come and to eat of the bread of life, therefore, is the fruit of grace. And if thus, by the marvellous grace of God we have been made hungry, and have tasted the goodness of the bread of life, we may safely confront the question the Lord put before His disciples after the carnal multitude of Capernaum had departed from Him: "Will ye also go away?" For we will surely answer with Peter: "Lord, to whom shall we go? Thou hast the words of eternal life. And we believe and are sure that thou art that Christ, the Son of the living God!" John 6:67-69.

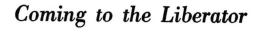

Coming to the Liberator

VI

Coming to the Liberator

*He hath sent me . . . to proclaim liberty
to the captives.*   —Isa. 61:1.

"Whosoever will may come." In our discussion of this
theme we asked the question: to whom must we come?
And the answer is: we must come to Jesus. But this
gave rise to the further question: and who is this Jesus
to whom we must come? And to this we have given
various answers, in order to discover whether man by
nature has the will to come to Him. Jesus is the revelation of the God of our salvation, and He is able to save to
the uttermost them that come to God by Him. The will
to come to Jesus, therefore, is motivated by the longing
to come to God. Christ is the Restgiver, and to them
that come to Him He promises eternal rest in the tabernacle
of God, the perfection of God's friendship and fellowship.
The will to come to Him presupposes that one seeks that
rest. Christ is the water and the bread of life, and the will
to come to Him means that one hungers and thirsts after
righteousness. Today we consider this Jesus to whom we
must come from still another aspect: He is also the true
Liberator, and He promises certain freedom to all that
come to Him.

More than once the Scriptures proclaim that Christ is
the Liberator and that in Him there is true freedom.

Already in the old dispensation He announced Himself through the prophet Isaiah as the one Whom the Lord had anointed to preach good tidings unto the meek, to bind up the brokenhearted, to proclaim liberty to the captives, and the opening of the prison to them that are bound. Isa. 61:1. And it was this passage which He read to an attentive and amazed audience in the synagogue of Nazareth, applying it to Himself in the words: "This day is this Scripture fulfilled in your ears." Lu. 4:16-21. Again, on the feast of the tabernacles He said to the Jews in Jerusalem: "If ye continue in my word, then are ye my disciples indeed; and ye shall know the truth, and the truth shall make you free. . . If the Son therefore shall make you free, ye shall be free indeed." John 8:31-36. Hence, it is the law of the Spirit of life in Christ Jesus that makes us free from the law of sin and death, Rom. 8:2. And through Him even the creature shall be delivered from the bondage of corruption into the glorious liberty of the children of God, Rom. 8:21. And where the Spirit of the Lord is, there is liberty, II Cor. 3:17. And they that come unto Him are admonished to stand in the liberty wherewith Christ hath made them free. Gal. 5:1. Christ is the true Liberator, and in Him there is freedom indeed!

Now, here it would seem, is a theme that appeals to the hearts of all men, and one might expect that all men would eagerly flock to this Jesus the Liberator that He might set them free. Are we not told that men thirst for freedom, and that liberty is more precious to them than life? Is it not said that all history is characterized by a fierce and determined struggle for freedom? Do we not hopefully look forward to the so-called four freedoms, freedom from fear, freedom from want, freedom of speech, and freedom of worship? And are we not enduring all the misery and destruction and bloodshed of the present world-conflict in order to attain to, and to secure unto ourselves that much coveted prize of freedom? Well, then, Christ promises all this! He announces Himself as the perfect Liberator. O, yes, He promises freedom from want, and that, too, from absolutely all want of body and of soul! He promises freedom from fear, and that, too, from all fear, the deepest and most universal cause of fear not excepted, that of death and hell. He promises freedom of speech in the true and highest sense of the word, and freedom of religion and worship that can never be shackled. And, mark you, He promises not only freedom *from* something, negatively, but His promise is of positive freedom. From want unto everlasting satisfaction and abundance, from fear unto perfect confidence and peace, from oppression unto complete liberty of conscience, from deepest misery unto highest bliss, from horrible death unto everlasting life, He promises to set us free! And He proffers this liberty as a free gift. You have nothing to sacrifice for it; you need not work or fight for this liberty; you need not go through the agony of war to attain to this liberty. He realizes this perfect liberty all alone! If the Son shall make you free, ye will be free indeed!

Yet, paradoxical though it may seem, men who fight to the death for freedom do not want true liberty, and will not come to Jesus. On both occasions we already mentioned on which the Lord proclaimed Himself as the Liberator, the Jews rejected Him, became incensed against Him, and wanted to kill Him. In Nazareth, though they admitted that He was a gracious speaker, they had it in their hearts to say to Him: "Physician, heal thyself." And when the Lord insisted, they became filled with wrath, and would have cast Him down the precipice, had He not miraculously shaken them off.   And in Jerusalem, the Jews denied that they were in bondage, called Him a Samaritan, said that He had a devil, and took up stones to kill him, but again the Lord easily escaped out of their hands, even going through the midst of them.   John 8:48 ff.   Nor is it different today.   Men rather strive and fight to the death for their own conception, their carnal and impossible conception of liberty, than to be liberated into the freedom with which Christ sets us free.

But why?

Why did men, who ostensibly were proud of their freedom, reject, seek to kill, and finally crucify Him Who proclaimed liberty to the captives?   And why do men, who claim that they highly prize liberty, and fight for their freedom, always crucify this Liberator afresh?   What is this freedom, which men despise?

We must understand that freedom is not, first of all, and in its deepest sense a relation of man to man, but of man to God.   Nor is it a mere external relationship, state, or condition: it is a matter of the heart of man.   And again liberty is not a state in which a man can do as *he* pleases, but it is a spiritual virtue according to which it pleases him to do the will of God.   Any creature is free that, according to the impulse of its inner nature, can live and move within the limits of the law of God ordained for that creature.   The eagle soars high into the sky, quite in harmony with its nature, and with the law of God for the eagle. Put the king of birds into a cage, or clip its wings, and it is no longer free.   The tree, on the other hand, thrives in the soil, and is free when it is firmly planted and is able to strike its roots into the ground.   Uproot it, and it is no longer free.   Now, man is a moral creature.   He has a rational nature. And the law of God, the living will of God, that is in harmony with man's nature is to love the Lord his God with all his heart, and with all his mind, and with all his soul, and with all his strength, and thus to live in the sphere of God's covenant of friendship. And that man is free who has the right, and who is able and willing to live in the sphere of that love.

For the sinner this means that liberty is freedom from sin! And this is the freedom Christ proclaimed. And he was not concerned about any other freedom. In fact, He was quite radical about this. He insisted that no freedom is possible, unless a man be free from sin. There is no real freedom from want, there is no possibility of freedom from fear, there is no freedom of thought, or of speech, or of worship, unless the sinner be liberated from the shackles of sin. For "whosoever sinneth is a slave of sin," John 8:34. And He denied that man is able to liberate himself. Only when He, the Son of God, makes him free, he shall be free indeed. Where the Spirit of the Lord is, there, and there alone is liberty. Outside of the sphere of that Spirit there is nothing but bondage.

Let us clearly understand this. The sinner is in bondage to sin. And this implies, first of all that he is guilty, sentenced to spiritual death, from which he has no right to be liberated. Consequently, his whole nature became corrupt. His mind became darkened, his will perverse, all his inclinations and desires polluted with sin. He is motivated by enmity of God. For "the carnal mind is enmity against God: for it is not subject to the law of God, neither indeed can be." Rom. 8:7. That is man's misery. He is a slave of sin, not in the sense that sin is a compelling force from without which he cannot escape, so that he commits sin against his will. On the contrary, he is free to sin. He has his delight in sin. But he is shackled from within. His will is in bondage. He will not love God, he cannot will to love God, he is incapable of seeking and willing and performing that which is good. Sin is the ruling power within him. It is enthroned in his heart, whence are all the issues of life. And under the dominion of sin he is pursued by the fear of death through all his life!

What, then, must be done to liberate that sinner? First of all, it is evident that he must be redeemed. Being a legal slave of sin, being condemned to sin's bondage, the price for his liberation must be paid. And this means that the guilt of his sin must be atoned, must be completely blotted out, and that he must be pronounced righteous, worthy of freedom and life, at the bar of divine justice. The justice of God against sin must be fully satisfied. He that would make man free must be able to bring the perfect sacrifice for sin, to bear the wrath of God, and to taste all the misery of death and hell, in perfect love of God. He must willingly enter into deepest desolation for God's righteousness' sake, and on the very bottom of hell he must say: "I love Thee, O my God! I have come here to do Thy will! Thy law is my delight even here!" By such an act of atonement he will obtain the *right* to liberate the sinner. But he must also actually set the sinner free. He must be able to enter into man's very heart, dethrone the power of sin, enthrone himself, cut the shackles of sin, remove the enmity against God, and fill the heart with a new love of God so that the sinner repents, hates all sin, and has new delight in the will of God. Thus redeemed, and thus delivered from the bondage of sin, the sinner is truly free. His heart is free, his will and mind are free; he is free from all fear, free from want, and in true freedom he may again worship the Lord his God, and serve Him only!

That Liberator is Christ! He does not merely *proclaim* freedom. He does not *instruct* us in the knowledge of freedom. He does not *show* us the way to freedom. No; He, the Christ of the Scriptures, the Son of God come in the likeness of sinful flesh, though without sin, Who died on Calvary, Who arose on the third day, Who ascended up on high leading captivity captive, and Who has all power in heaven and on earth, Christ, the quickening Spirit, He has the right to liberate us, He has the power to set us free, and He actually delivers us from the dominion of sin, and makes us partakers of the glorious liberty of the children of God!

He could pay the price of our redemption. For He is eternally free Himself. He is the very Son of God. And the Son is free, even in our flesh. He had no sin. He was not defiled. There was no possibility that He would ever sin. He was free in the highest sense of the word. He loved the Father with His whole being. And freely, by an act of perfect obedience, motivated by the love of God, He descended into the lowest parts of the earth, into deepest hell, and humbled Himself even unto death, yea, unto the death of the cross. And in all his suffering, agonies of hell, reproach and shame, He was never in bondage. He was ever free. He loved the Father. He was the perfect servant. Even when He crawled in the dust of the garden, even when in the darkest moment of His humiliation He cried out: "My God, my God, why hast thou forsaken me?" He was still free, and willingly fulfilled all righteousness, satisfying the justice of God against sin!

That is the mystery of the cross!

That is why the word of the cross is foolishness to them that perish! O, how different from man's efforts to attain to freedom is Christ's way! Man seeks power, a sign, human wisdom. Man marshals mighty armies, invents instruments of destruction, defies death, to attain to and to defend his freedom. Christ fights the battle all alone! And how strangely he fights! In the garden He is utterly amazed, in fear of death. This Liberator is bound, lets Himself be bound, refusing the power of the sword, in His battle for freedom! He does not protest when they abuse Him; He does not defend His cause when they accuse Him; He does not open His mouth when they condemn Him to death! He gives His back to the smiters! He heals the wounds of the enemy! He allows Himself to be stretched upon the tree, to be nailed to the cross. When they challenge Him to liberate Himself and to come down from the cross, He does not reply. A Liberator that Himself is bound, and completely overcome by the power of the enemy!

Yet, so it must be. For His battle was not against flesh and blood, but against the powers of the devil, sin and death. And these could be overcome only by the act of perfect obedience, the obedience of love, of true freedom, even unto the end. And by that act, Christ obtained for us the right to perfect liberty, freedom from sin, from the wrath of God from the curse of the law, freedom unto eternal righteousness, life and glory in the sphere of the perfect love of God! And having obtained remission of sins, perfect righteousness, and the right to deliver us and set us free, He was raised in glory, and was exalted at the right hand of God, endowed with all power to effect our liberation from the dominion of fear, of misery, of sin, and death!

But how do we become partakers of the freedom Christ has purchased for us? O, yes, we must come to Him as our only Liberator. And whosoever will may come! Nor shall anyone ever come to Him in vain. They that come to Him will surely be set free. But how? Who are they that are willing to come to Him that they may be liberated by His wondrous grace? Is it thus, perhaps, that this Christ stands outside of the door of our prison of sin and death, and from there proclaims to us that He has the right and the power to deliver to us, and that He is willing to set us free, if only we will open the door, and let Him in? But God forbid! Let us not forget that the sinner's heart and will are in bondage to sin. He is a willing slave. He delights in his bondage. He despises liberty. He will not come to Christ as the Liberator that He may set him free. If Christ must wait for the sinner, no sinner can be saved!

But thanks be to God! Christ is first! He is the quickening Spirit! And by that Spirit He enters into our hearts, and in a way far too wonderful for us to comprehend, He dethrones the power of sin, He cuts the shackles of corruption, He liberates the heart and the will and the mind by the power of His marvellous grace. And then He calls, calls through the gospel, yet always it is He Himself that calls, and He appeals to that heart, and to that mind, and to that will that have been renewed by His grace. And then you hear the voice of Jesus say: "Come unto me, and I will set you free" And you see your real bondage, and you repent of your sin, and you long to be set free, and you cry out: "God, be merciful to me, a sinner!" That is the cry of freedom! And you flee to your Liberator, and He receives you. And He makes you partake of His perfect righteousness by faith and spreads abroad in your heart the love of God. And there descends into your heart peace instead of fear, hope instead of terror, love instead of enmity, life instead of death, heaven instead of hell. You have been made free for ever! And you look forward in the joy of hope to the final realization of the glorious liberty of the children of God

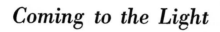

Coming to the Light

VII

Coming to the Light

I am the light of the world . . .
—JOHN 8:12.

ON that same feast of the tabernacles in Jerusalem, where
our Saviour presented Himself as the water of life,
and called men to come unto Him, and drink; and where
He proclaimed Himself as the Son that would set men
free, so that they might be free indeed; He also presented
Himself as the light of the world. "Then spake Jesus
again unto them, saying, I am the light of the world: he
that followeth me shall not walk in darkness, but shall
have the light of life." John 8:12. A bold statement indeed! No wonder people were amazed at His doctrine!
No wonder they gave Him testimony that His speech was
different from that of the scribes and Pharisees and that
He spake with authority. A very bold man may probably
claim that he is able to shed some light in the darkness
of this world, or that he can point out the light. But the
Lord does not say that He will shed some light, that He
will instruct men to enlighten them, that He will show
them the way to the light, but that He *is* the light! He
claims, not that He is *a* light among others, but that He
is *the* light, the only light, so that outside of Him, and
apart from Him there is nothing but darkness. And He
insists, not that He is able to act as a light in some spheres

or departments of life, but that He is the light of the whole world! And He promises unconditionally to them that follow Him that they shall not walk in darkness but shall have light, even the light of life! It is evident, then, that whoever would come to Jesus must approach Him and follow Him as the light of the world. The will to come to the Saviour is motivated by the desire and mighty longing to come to the light!

More often the Scriptures speak of Christ as the light. In John 1:4-9 we read: "In him was life; and the life was the light of men. And the light shineth in darkness; and the darkness comprehended it not. There was a man sent from God, whose name was John. The same came for a witness, to bear witness of the light, that all men through Him might believe. He was not that light, but was sent to bear witness of that Light. That was the true light, which lighteth every man coming into the world." And in John 3:19-21: "And this is the condemnation, that light is come into the world, and men loved darkness rather than light, because their deeds were evil. For every one that doeth evil hateth the light, neither cometh to the light, lest his deeds should be reproved. But he that doeth truth cometh to the light, that his deeds may be made manifest that they are wrought in God." And again: "I am come a light into the world, that whosoever believeth on me should not abide in darkness." John 12:46.

In these passages various elements draw our attention. First of all, it is evident that they teach us that the world is in darkness, whatever may be the meaning of this figure. Secondly, they insist that Christ is the sole light that is able to dissipate this darkness of the world. In the third place they present men in themselves as loving darkness rather than the light, so that they will not come to Christ as the Light. Fourthly, this very fact, that light is come into the world and men refuse to come to it, is their condemnation. They are exposed and judged by the light as lovers of darkness. And, lastly they teach us that only they that are doers of the truth come to the light.

We must try to understand, therefore, what is the implication of the Scriptural figure of "light," and of its antithesis "darkness." For we understand that when the Lord announces Himself as the light of the world He uses figurative language. And a rich and beautiful figure it is, indeed. In nature, physical light, the light which God called into being on the first day of creation week, is no doubt the indispensable condition for the existence, movement and life of all the rest of the world. Light is movement, vibration, heat, fellowship, communion, revelation, is itself life. Hence, when used in a spiritual sense in Holy Writ, it has a rich significance. It denotes spiritual, ethical perfection and life. That this is true is evident from the several passages in Scripture where the figure is employed, as well as from the use of its opposite and antithesis *darkness*. When the apostle John writes "that God is light, and there is no darkness in him at all," he does not merely express that there is knowledge in God, and He knows Himself with an infinite perfect knowledge, so that nothing is hid from Him, but also that He is the implication of all perfections. God is infinitely good and there is no evil in Him. He is the holy One, and there is no corruption in Him at all. He is righteousness, justice, truth, wisdom, knowledge, love and life. And in the perfection of this light the triune God lives an infinitely perfect life of eternal fellowship and friendship, of the Father, through the Son, and in the Holy Spirit. Light, therefore, denotes all spiritual ethical perfection goodness, holiness, righteousness, wisdom and knowledge, while darkness implies the very opposite of these, corruption and defilement, evil and iniquity, unrighteousness and the lie, sin and death. "If we say that we have fellowship with him, and walk in darkness, we lie, and do not the truth: But if we walk in the light, as he is in the light, we have fellowship with one another, and the blood of Jesus Christ his Son cleanseth us from all sin." I John 1:6 7. Light is the truth, darkness is the lie; light is the love of God, darkness is enmity against Him; light is righteousness, darkness is iniquity; light is purity, holiness, consecration to God, darkness is corruption, filth, rebellion; light is wisdom, darkness is folly; light is life in the fellowship with God, darkness is death, the desolation of being forsaken of Him in wrath.

Now, when our Lord announces Himself as the light of the world it is evident that He speaks of the world of men, of the entire human race. And it is also plain that thereby He characterizes that world of men as being in darkness apart from Him. And this is corroborated by many other passages of Holy Writ. The apostle Paul writes that we were sometimes darkness, but that we are now light in the Lord, Eph. 5:8; and he speaks of the rulers of the darkness of this world, Eph. 6:12. Those that are translated into the kingdom of God's Son are delivered from the power of darkness, Col. 1:13; and they are called out of darkness into his marvellous light, I Pet. 2:9.

Surely, this is not a very flattering evaluation of the world, and of men as they are by nature. And they that proclaim this truth consistently must expect much contradiction. And superficially considered, it would appear too harsh, too radical a judgment to say that the whole world is darkness. What? must this entire world with its imposing civilization, with its progress and invention, its science and philosophy, its culture and art, be condemned as darkness? How would you explain all the mighty works of man, if all is under the dominion of the darkness of the lie and corruption? And is there not a good deal of righteousness and justice, of love and charity, of nobility and self-sacrifice, of truth and honor in this world? O, it may be granted that there is something wrong, and even that there is a good deal of darkness and corruption among men. But to say that men are darkness, and that apart from Christ there is no light at all —that is altogether too severe and radical a judgment upon our modern world!

Yet, such is exactly the judgment of Scripture. And unless we accept this judgment, we will never come to the Christ of the Scriptures.

Let us try to understand this truth. God created man in the light, and He endowed him with many excellent gifts. He was gifted with the light of the eye, whereby he could perceive the world about him. He was created with the light of understanding, whereby he was capable of understanding and knowing himself and the handiwork of God. And he was created with the spiritual light of the love of God, so that he could know his God rightly, be consecrated to Him with his whole being, walk before Him in righteousness, and live in the fellowship of friendship with his Creator, the ever blessed God. He had the light of life. He was created in the image of God. Serving God he walked in the light. But he plunged himself into darkness. In willful disobedience, he rejected the Word of God, and accepted and followed the lie of the devil. The result was that he became guilty, worthy of death, object of the wrath of God. Having separated himself from God's fellowship, he became darkened in his understanding, so that he loved the lie; perverse of will, rebellious and obdurate of heart, corrupt and defiled in all his desires. That is his darkness. The light of the image of God in him was extinguished, and instead his whole nature was enveloped in the darkness of ignorance and foolishness, of unrighteousness and unholiness. His love of God was perverted into enmity. And having thus become darkness he walks in darkness.

It is true, there are in man the remnants of natural light: he is still a rational moral creature. And by this light he accomplishes all the mighty works which we see the natural man in the modern world of culture and civilization perform. In this light he also knows that God is, and that He must be glorified and served. He discerns the difference between good and evil, and he understands that the law of God is good for him, and that to violate that law means destruction. Hence, he tries to adapt his life outwardly to that law and speaks of righteousness and justice, of truth and honesty. But even so he loves the darkness, and he walks in it. "Because that when they knew God, they glorified him not as God, neither were thankful; but became vain in their imaginations, and their foolish heart was darkened. Professing themselves to be wise they became fools, and changed the glory of the incorruptible God into an image made like unto corruptible man, and to birds, and to fourfooted beasts, and creeping things." Rom. 1:21-23. "They are all under sin. As it is written, There is none righteous, no, not one: There is none that understandeth, there is none that seeketh after God. They are all gone out of the way, they are together become unprofitable; there is none that doeth good, no, not one. Their throat is an open sepulchre; with their tongues they have used deceit; the poison of asps is under their lips: Whose mouth is full of cursing and bitterness: Their feet are swift to shed blood: Destruction and misery are in their ways: And the way of peace have they not known: There is no fear of God before their eyes."

Such is man. And this is true of every man. And the
truth of this becomes glaringly evident in our modern world
of death and destruction, of hatred and greed, of adultery
and lust. Nor is there a way out as far as man is concerned. Neither education nor reform, neither culture nor
civilization, neither philosophy nor science can lead man
out of the darkness. All these move themselves in the
sphere of darkness and stand in the service of sin and
corruption. And the inevitable end is destruction and
eternal desolation.

But Christ is the light that is able to overcome and
dispel this darkness. He is the light of the world, not
because He is the greatest reformer, or educator, or moralist,
or character builder, or scientist, or philosopher that ever
was; or because He did more than any other to save our
civilization; or even because He was a religious genius
with a profound God-consciousness. All such modern dis-
tortions of Christ simply drag Him into our darkness. But
He is from above. He is the Son of God, co-eternal with
the Father and the Holy Ghost, God of God, Light of
Light, come into the flesh, Immanuel, God with us. He
has light in Himself. And as such He entered into our
world of darkness, and penetrated even into its deepest
depth. For He took our sins upon Himself, and bore in
our stead the wrath of God. And with the load of our
sins upon His mighty shoulders He descended into the
dark abode of death and hell, and in the perfect obedience
of love offered the sacrifice that obtained for us eternal
righteousness. And thus He broke through the hopeless
darkness of death into the light of His glorious resurrection.
And as the Light of the world He ascended up on high,
and received the promise of the Spirit, in order that by
this Spirit He may dispel the darkness of sin and death,

and cause the light of the glorious gospel of God, the light
of righteousness and life, the light of hope and eternal joy
to shine in our hearts. And thus it is realized what was
prophesied in the days of old: "The people which sat in
darkness saw a great light; and to them which sat in the
region and shadow of death light is sprung up." Matt. 4:16.

And when thus the Light of the world shines in our
hearts, we are delivered from the power of darkness, called
out of darkness into the marvellous light of God, and what
the apostle writes in Eph. 5:8 is realized in us: "For ye
were sometimes darkness, but now are ye light in the Lord."
In principle the believer is a new creature, a child of light.
The old things of sin and death, of iniquity and corruption,
of enmity against God and hatred of one another, have
passed away; behold, all things have become new. Drawn
by the light, he follows the light, and walks in it. He repents of sin, and longs after righteousness; he has a new
joy in God, and finds that in the keeping of His precepts
there is a great reward. He fights the good fight of faith,
and represents the cause of the Son of God in this world.
Always he puts off the old man and puts on the new man,
which after God is created in righteousness and true holiness. Reflecting the light of the Son of God, he, too, is
the light of the world, and he lets his light shine that men
may see his good works, and glorify his Father who is
in heaven. And he looks forward to the perfect day, when
he shall be completely delivered from all the remnants of
darkness and walk in the light of God and of the Lamb
for evermore!

Whosoever will may come to Christ as the Light of the
world, may follow Him, and may surely experience the
truth of His Word: "he that followeth me shall not walk
in darkness, but shall have the light of life."

But how shall a man that is darkness come to the light? Or how shall a sinner that loves the darkness rather than the light even will to come and to follow Him? O, how impossible this is! Yet, this is exactly the distortion of the gospel that is proclaimed by many in our day. The darkness according to them, must come to the Light, in order that the darkness may be dispelled. Christ, the Light of the world, is exhibited by some preacher to men that are in darkness. And He is willing to enlighten them with the light of life, if they will only let the light shine in their hearts. But if they are unwilling the Light of the world cannot penetrate to dispel their darkness. And so they preach a mighty darkness and a powerless Light!

But thanks be to God, the Light of the world does not shine by the grace and good will of the darkness; it is sovereign. It is not dependent on the will of the sinner: it is irresistible. It is not contingent upon the begging and pleading and contortions of a modern hawker of Jesus, but sends its piercing and illuminating rays whithersoever it wills. The darkness does not come to the light, but the Light shines into the darkness through the Spirit of grace, exposes the darkness, convicts of sin, draws into the light of life. And then the sinner comes and follows. Nor does he ever finally return to the darkness. Forever the Light continues to shine and to draw him on, until at last he enters into the city that is illuminated by the glory of God, and whose light is the Lamb! There he shall see face to face and know even as he is known!

Coming to the Resurrection

VIII

Coming to the Resurrection

I am the resurrection and the life.
—JOHN 11:25.

SALVATION is resurrection from the dead. This statement is not to be understood as having reference only to the final, bodily resurrection in glory to which believers look forward as the ultimate realization of their hope, but to the whole of salvation. Also the salvation that is the inheritance of believers by faith in Christ here in the world is very really resurrection from the dead. He that is saved by faith is raised from the dead, and this resurrection will be perfected in the day of Christ, when this mortal shall put on immortality, and the last enemy shall be destroyed.

That this is true may easily be demonstrated from Scripture. Christ Jesus is the revelation of the God of our salvation that quickens the dead. In creation He reveals Himself as the One that calls the things that are not as if they were; in Christ He is known as the One that raises the dead. Rom. 4:17. Hence "if thou shalt confess with they mouth the Lord Jesus, and shalt believe in thine heart that God hath raised him from the dead, thou shalt be saved." Rom. 10:9. And therein, that God raised Christ from the dead, and set Him at His own right hand in heavenly places, He revealed the exceeding greatness of His power to usward who believe, Eph. 1:19 20. And even now it is true that God who is rich in mercy, for His great love wherewith He loved us, even when we were dead in sins, hath quickened us together with Christ, and hath raised us up together with Him, Eph. 2:4-6. "Wherefore he saith, Awake thou that sleepest, and arise from the dead, and Christ shall give thee light." Eph. 5:14. And the Lord Himself declares: "Verily, verily, I say unto you The hour is coming and now is, when the dead shall hear the voice of the Son of God: and they that hear shall live." John 5:25.

Hence, Christ stands before us in the gospel narratives as the resurrection. In all the mighty signs and wonders which He performed, and by which He cured the sick, opened the eyes of the blind, made the deaf to hear, and the lame to leap with joy, He revealed Himself as the resurrection. Especially is this true, of course of those signs by which He recalled the dead to this earthly life, the mightiest of which is the raising of Lazarus. Yet these were but signs, and they were all fulfilled when He broke the bonds of death and hell, and appeared in glory, Victor over all the power of the grave and corruption. Then His word to Martha, the sister of Lazarus, was fully and mightily realized: "I am the resurrection and the life: he that believeth in me, though he were dead, yet shall he live: And whosoever liveth and believeth in me shall never die." John 11:25, 26.

This truth, that salvation is resurrection from the dead, and that, too, through Christ Who is the resurrection, is of great importance for a true understanding of the general theme we are discussing: "whosoever will may come." It should help us to find the correct answer to the question whether the sinner has in himself the will to come to Jesus. For there is in this truth a threefold implication, which we must briefly discuss. First of all, if salvation is nothing less than resurrection from the dead, it should be evident that before a sinner is saved he is very really in the power of death. Secondly, we ought to consider what it means that Christ is the resurrection. And, finally, it is plain, that the dead sinner must be brought into contact with the living Christ, the resurrection, in order to be saved.

The sinner apart from Christ, we said is dead. This is not only the plain presupposition of the truth that salvation is resurrection from the dead, but this is also clearly taught in Scripture throughout. The sentence of God upon the sinner is: "in the day that thou eatest thereof thou shalt surely die." Gen. 2:17. And that sentence was executed literally and on the spot, so that the natural man is now dead through trespasses and sins, Eph. 2:1.

But what does it mean that the sinner is dead? What, then, is this death in whose power the sinner is held, and from which he can never deliver himself? Death, we understand, is no annihilation. Nor is it a state of unconscious existence. It is rather a state of corruption, suffering, and misery under the avenging justice and terrible wrath of God. It concerns our whole being. In a spiritual sense death is corruption of the soul and of the spirit of man, so that all the powers of his soul work in opposition to God. In death man's understanding is darkened, so that he does not know the good but loves the lie, and he is utterly devoid of true wisdom. His will is perverted, so that he does not, and cannot desire and choose for true righteousness and holiness in the love of God. All his inclinations are impure and defiled, so that he lusts after iniquity. In death, man's heart, whence are the issues of life, instead of being filled with the love of God, is moved by enmity against him. And this is indeed, the state of the natural man, of the sinner apart from Christ. He is carnal. His nature is after the flesh. And "they that are after the flesh, do mind the things of the flesh . . . for to be carnally minded is death . . . because the carnal mind is enmity against God: for it is not subject to the law of God, neither indeed can be." In the physical sense, death is the corruption and disintegration of the organism of the body. And also unto this death man was delivered up immediately after the fall. The power of death operates in his members, reveals itself in many diseases and defects of the body, and finally drags man to the place of utter corruption. And so, he very really was plunged into eternal death, the state of complete desolation of soul and body in hell, for God's fierce anger pursues him, and there is no way out.

It is important that we bear in mind that this state of death in which man plunged himself by his willful disobedience is a legal state i. e. it is retribution, it is punishment, it is the execution of a divine death sentence. It is not "natural" for man to be dead, and to die. Nor is it a mere, natural result of his sin. It is true, the wages of sin is death, but only because divine justice causes sin to pay that wage. It is God that kills. Sin is the transgression of God's law. It is rebellion. It is ethical evil. It is rebellion against the living God. And God is good. He is just. He allows no creature to deny His goodness with impunity. He maintains himself in all the glory of His goodness, of His divine perfection, of His righteousness and justice, His truth and holiness, over against the sinner that departs from Him, and raises the rebellious fist against Him. He reveals His unchangeable perfection to the sinner by making him unspeakably miserable by causing him to experience that there is no life and joy apart from God. He pursues that sinner everywhere and constantly in His wrath, until he sinks away in everlasting desolation. God is the terror of the sinner. God, from Whom the sinner can never escape, from Whom he cannot hide himself in all the wide creation, Whom he may deny in his folly, but Whom he, nevertheless, meets at every step, and with Whom he will have to do unto unending ages of ages,—that God is against him, and causes him to experience His fierce and holy anger! That is death!

Now, Christ is the resurrection! This means that He is the power that overcomes, and completely destroys, our death. And as the cause of our death is the righteous and holy wrath of God, it implies that Christ is the power whereby we are translated from this state of divine anger and burning wrath, under which we pine and die, into a state of favor and grace with the living God. And as the ground of the wrath of God that is against us and pursues us unto death, is our sin and guilt, the truth that Christ is the resurrection means that He is the blotting out of our sin, the obliteration of the handwriting of our sin, and that He is our perfect and everlasting righteousness with God. Christ is our resurrection because He removes the cause of eternal death and misery, namely sin; and, clothing us with perfect righteousness, makes us the proper objects of God's blessed favor. And as there is death in God's wrath, so there is life in His favor!

But it means more than this. That Christ is the resurrection also means that He is the quickening power, and that in Him there is life out of death. Life is the operation and action of our whole being, of body and soul, of heart and mind and will and all our desires, in harmony with God. Just as death is enmity against God, so life is to love Him with all our heart and mind and soul and strength. Just as death is darkness, so life is light. Just as death is folly, ignorance, the lie, so life is true wisdom, knowledge of God, the truth. Just as death is perversion of the will, so life is the harmony of the will with the will of God. Just as death is corruption, impurity, defilement of all our desires, so life is purity of heart, the longing after the living God. Just as death is the state of being forsaken of God in His wrath, so life is the most intimate fellowship with God in His blessed favor. Just as death is unspeakable misery and desolation, so life is purest joy and blessedness. This is life eternal, that they might know thee the only true God, and Jesus Christ whom thou hast sent, John 17:3. And Christ is that life out of death! He is light out of darkness, righteousness out of unrighteousness, truth out of the lie, knowledge of God out of ignorance, wisdom out of folly, glory out of shame, hope out of despair, joy out of misery, heaven out of hell! He is the resurrection and the life!

One more observation must be made in this connection. He is the resurrection. And resurrection is not a return to a former state but a passing through death into a more abundant life than was ever known before. It is, first of all, an entering into a completely victorious life, that is for ever delivered from death. In the first Adam there was a life that could be lost. He was mortal. In the last Adam there is a life that is victorious over death, that can never be lost. Death has no more dominion over Him. The shadow of death can never touch Him any more that is the resurrection. And, in the second place, resurrection-life is heavenly: it is the highest possible realization of the blessed fellowship with God, a seeing face to face, and a knowing even as we are known in the heavenly tabernacle of God. That Christ is the resurrection signifies that He is the power that raises us from the depth of hell into the glory of heaven!

It is the Christ of the Scriptures Who is the resurrection. None other! Ah, how miserable are the substitutes modernism offers for this Christ of the Scriptures! How absolutely devoid of power are those substitutes to save out of death! Or of what avail to the dead is a dead Christ? Of what avail to the dead sinner is a wonderful teacher, a good example, a man of principle, a Christ for whom we must make this world a better place to live in? The Christ of the Scriptures is the resurrection! He is such first of all, because He is the very Son of God, co-eternal with the Father and the Holy Ghost. From everlasting to everlasting He is God! And as the eternal Son He is life, and He has life in Himself. To Martha He said: "I am the resurrection and the life." And to the Jews in Jerusalem he said on another occasion: "For as the Father hath life in himself; so hath he given to the Son to have life in himself." Exactly because He is the life, and because He has life in Himself, He could be the resurrection. And He actually is the resurrection, because He entered into our deepest death, and destroyed it for ever. For, He was ordained from before the foundation of the world to be the Head of His Church. And as such He became flesh, and united Himself with us, that He might taste death in our stead and in our behalf. Our sins He took upon Himself. The whole burden of our iniquity He bore. And with the load of our sins upon His mighty shoulders He willingly descended into the darkness of death, bore the wrath of God in perfect obedience, blotted out all our guilt, and obtained for us eternal righteousness. And thus He fought the battle with death, and overcame the enemy. Being the life and having life in Himself, it was impossible that death shrould hold Him. The shackles of death He broke, and He issued forth into life immortal. But still more. For He ascended up on high, and received the promise of the Holy Spirit, thus becoming the quickening Spirit, in order that He might be the resurrection for all His own. Thus the Son of God, Who has life in Himself, come in the likeness of sinful flesh, and for sin, took away the cause of our eternal death and misery, was delivered for our transgressions and raised for our justification, and is become the true resurrection, by Whom we may be quickened from death unto everlasting life!

It is plain, then that we must come to Him, to Jesus, Who is the resurrection and the life. Outside of Him, there is nothing but death; in Him there is life out of death. It is evident that, in order to be saved, we must have contact, a living contact with Him, in order that the power of His glorious life may destroy the dominion of death in us, and we may be translated from death into life. For, as the Lord said to Martha, when He was about to recall Lazarus from the grave: "He that believeth in me, though he were dead, yet shall he live: and he that liveth and believeth in me shall never die." We must come, therefore to Him, in order that out of Him we may draw life for ever.

And "whosoever will may come." O, yes, there is no exception to this. If you come to Christ as the resurrection and the life, you shall never be put to shame. No one ever came to Him, nor shall anyone ever come to Him, that did not receive righteousness and life!

But again we ask the question: how shall we come to Jesus, the resurrection? How shall sinners that are dead in themselves seek and establish contact with that power of life? Shall preachers be sent to them to proclaim to them that Jesus is the resurrection, and that He is willing to impart His life to them, that He is waiting for them somewhere, that He is earnestly begging them to come to Him, that He is watching for the signal on their part that He may go ahead and quicken them? Shall we say to men that He can do no more, and that if the dead will not come to Him, the resurrection will never come to them? And shall we thus persuade the dead to take action at once, before it is too late? That is, in substance, the gospel, or rather, the corruption of the gospel that is being proclaimed rather generally in our day. But how absurd! And how utterly impossible! You might as well proclaim that on the day of the final resurrection Christ will send some so-called evangelist to persuade the dead to come out of their graves, that they may be glorified! Such a perversion of the gospel denies, after all, that man is really dead, and that Christ is really the resurrection. It preaches a death that is more powerful than the resurrection; a resurrection that must fail if death does not give its consent!

But thanks be to God, the quickening action proceeds freely and sovereignly from the resurrection! Christ is first! "The hour is coming and now is, when the dead shall hear the voice of the Son of God: and they that hear shall live!" Mark you well, it is the mighty voice of the Son of God that speaks. He calls, and Who shall resist? His mighty Word is quickening. By His Word the dead are raised. The resurrection comes to the dead, before the dead come to the resurrection. And when they have been quickened, called out of their sleep of death, they come, humbly, willingly, by the action of their God given faith, and consciously draw out of Him righteousness and life for ever! And they look forward to the hour, when they shall hear His voice once more, calling them out of the dust of the earth into the glory of the final resurrection!

The Act of Coming

IX

The Act of Coming

*All that the Father giveth me shall come
to me; and him that cometh to me I
will in no wise cast out.* —JOHN 6:37.

THUS far, in our discussion of the theme *Whosoever
will may come, we* tried to find an answer to the question: to whom must we come? The answer is: we must
come to Jesus. And as we elaborated upon the meaning
and implications of this answer, we found that the Scriptures present Jesus as the revelation of the God of our
salvation, as the giver of rest, the water and the bread
of life, the liberator, the light of the world, the resurrection
and the life. The will to come to Him, therefore, must
be motivated by the desire to come to God, the longing
for rest, a hunger and thirst after righteousness, a yearning
after true freedom, love of the light, and the earnest desire
to be delivered from death, and to be quickened unto a
new life.

But what does it mean to come to Jesus? We have
become so accustomed to hear this phrase that we probably
consider it quite superfluous to give ourselves a clear
account of its meaning. Yet, it is important that we answer
this question. Before a person can heed the call to come
to Jesus, and in order to be sure that he did obey that

call, he must have some understanding of its implications. Now, it should be plain that the phrase *coming to Jesus* is somewhat figurative. In the physical sense no one can come to Christ. When He was on earth, and preached in the cities and villages of the land of Canaan, it was, indeed, possible to follow up the call to come to Him literally, to approach Him, to speak to Him, and to touch Him. However, even then, if anyone would have understood the call in this literal, physical sense, the Lord would no doubt, have instructed him that such a coming could be of no avail, that one must come to Him spiritually, and that, before this could be fully realized, He must go away, through death and resurrection, in order that He might return in the Spirit, and thus become the bread of life for all that come to Him. When the bread seeking multitude at Capernaum murmured at His saying that they must eat His flesh and drink His blood, in order to have true life, He said unto them: "Doth this offend you? What and if ye shall see the Son of man ascend up where he was before? It is the Spirit that quickeneth; the flesh profiteth nothing." John 6:61-63. To come to Jesus, therefore, is a spiritual approach to Christ, the Son of God come into the flesh, crucified and slain, raised on the third day, and exalted in the highest heavens, as He is revealed in the gospel.

And well may we pause for a moment to consider what is implied in this act of coming to Jesus. What is implied in this spiritual approach to the Christ of the Scriptures? What does one do when he comes to Jesus? And how is it possible for a sinner to come to Him?

All the more peremptory it is to inquire into the meaning of coming to Jesus because of the abominable travesty of it that is presented by many a modern self-styled evangelist and revivalist. And it is high time that the Church, that is the custodian of the gospel, and to whom alone is given the commission to preach the Word, should raise her voice aloud in protest against the widely practised evil of hawking Jesus, and of presenting Him as the cheapest article on the religious market, that may either be procured or rejected by the sinner at will. To come to Jesus is, according to a very usual phrase, to accept Him as our personal Saviour. And this would not be so objectionable if it were not for all the misrepresentations that are connected with it. All emphasis is laid on that word "accept." One must accept Jesus, that is all. And to do this lies within the power of every sinner. On this acceptance of Jesus by the sinner everything depends. For this act on the sinner's part the Saviour must wait. It is the signal which the sinner gives Christ that He may go ahead and save him. It is the act whereby the sinner opens the door of his heart to a Christ that stands and knocks at that door, but who is unable to enter, unless the sinner permits Him. O, indeed, they admit that salvation is of grace, and some of these hawkers of salvation even prattle of sovereign grace; but this grace is, nevertheless, presented as enervated and paralyzed if the sinner refuses its saving operation!

And this gives rise to all the evils of which Arminianism gone wild affords daily demonstrations from pulpits and over the air. The sinner's power to accept or reject Jesus receives all the emphasis, and the result is that the act itself of coming to Christ is presented as something natural and very simple. All that is required of the sinner is to raise his hand, or to come to the front, or to kneel down by the radio, and repeat after the preacher: "I accept Jesus as my personal Saviour," and the matter is settled. If the sinner will only do this, the Holy Spirit will come into his heart and make him a new born child of God. And seeing that the thing is so natural, and that it lies within the power of every sinner to accept Jesus, very *natural* means are employed to persuade the sinner to take this step, and to let Jesus come into his heart. Hence, the highly sensational altar call, climaxing the sermon, in which the preacher is done with expository preaching, and can say what he wants. All that is calculated to arouse mere human emotions is now brought into play. Sentimentalism replaces the sound preaching of the Word. The audience is asked to bow their heads in silent prayer. The organ softly plays, or the choir gently sings: "Softly and tenderly Jesus is calling," or "Just as I am without one plea." And in the meantime the preacher begs and pleads, and with a voice full of emotion asks sinners to raise their hands, to come to the front, to let Jesus into their hearts, and to accept Him as their personal Saviour. He speaks of a God that begs for the privilege to come into their hearts, of a Holy Spirit that longs to make newborn children of God of them, and of a sinner upon whom alone depends the decision of life and death, of hell and heaven, of the whole matter of salvation, and of the very glorw of God in Christ! And the result is as *natural* as the means that are employed. Instead of the new birth the emotions are aroused; a sentimental tear of self-pity is mistaken for true repentance; and a temporary elation of the soul is erroneously called joy in Christ!

The result is that churches that are built upon this unstable foundation of emotionalism are constantly in

need of more and greater emotional stir to maintain themselves, and to keep their auditoriums filled. Preachers
try to draw a crowd by announcing the most extraordinary
and silly sermon-topics. Besides, they are in need of
periodical revivals, and for this purpose some extra sensational evangelists, men or women, are employed, and their
coming is advertised in the daily papers and on billboards
with the promise of special thrills and extraordinary excite-
ment. And these revivalistic campaigns are said to be
successful. Hundreds and thousands of souls are converted
by these men. And it is to be feared, and the ultimate result usually shows that it was, indeed, by the preachers,
rather than by the Spirit of Christ that they were converted.

Against this evil of sentimentalism and freewillism gone
wild I raise my unqualified protest. There is no example
of it in the preaching of Christ and of the apostles. And
I would call upon the Church to return to sound preaching
and sound doctrine, to instruct young and old in the truth
of the gospel, and to preach a mighty Christ and a poor,
helpless sinner, a sinner that can come to Jesus only by
the power of His Spirit and grace! It is through such
preaching that Christ will gather His Church, and that
sinners will be saved and grow in the knowledge and
grace of our Lord Jesus Christ!

What is it, then, to come to Christ? It is a spiritual
act, not a mere natural deed. It is an act that proceeds
from the heart, whence are the issues of life; not from
the superficial and quickly changing emotions. It is an act
of the whole man: with all his heart and mind and will
and desires and strength one comes to Jesus. It is an
act, not of the natural man, but of the spiritual man; of

the one that is heavy laden and weary with sin, and seeks rest; of the one that hungers and thirsts after righteousness, and seeks the bread that never perishes, and the water of life; of the one that bemourns his darkness, and seeks the light; of the one that cries out of the depths of death for the resurrection. And being a spiritual act by a spiritual man, it does not condition grace, but is already the fruit of the grace of the Holy Spirit. It is an act, lastly, that is never finished, as if a man could say that years ago he came to Christ and that is the end of it; but that is the daily need and delight of the new man in Christ to perform. To these various aspects of the act of coming to Christ I would like to call your attention.

First of all, then, let us try to analyze the act of coming to Jesus itself. What does a man do, when he comes to the Christ of the Scriptures? I think that we may distinguish four elements or steps in this spiritual act which I will call: contrition, recognition, aspiration, and appropriation.

First of all, there is the element of contrition. This is a true sorrow after God, caused by the fact that man has obtained a true spiritual knowledge of sin as sin, and of himself as a sinner before the face of God. This does not mean merely that he knows and acknowledges that there is something wrong with him; nor that he is sorrowing because of the evil and bitter results of sin for himself; nor that he is sorry because of certain bad habits. No, this sorrow of true contrition goes to the root of the matter. It means that the sinner consciously stands before the bar of divine justice, that the pure and penetrating light of the righteousness of God exposes him in his true worth as a sinner, that in the light of inexorable justice he beholds himself, his nature, his work, his imaginary goodness, his piety and religion, and discovers that there is nothing good in him, that all is corruption, defilement, iniquity, rebellion, violation of God's law; that he hears the divine verdict of guilty, and the sentence of his condemnation. But it means more. It means, O wonder, that now he takes God's side in this judgment against himself and in his own condemnation, that he hates his own sin, acknowledges the justice of God's sentence, and prostrates himself before the bar of justice in dust and ashes. He sees that as sinner he cannot enter into God's fellowship, and confesses that as far as he is concerned there is no way out. He is filled with sorrow according to God!

Secondly, there is in the act of coming to Christ the element of recognition. By this I mean a true, spiritual knowledge of Jesus Christ as the revelation of the God of our salvation. I say, spiritual knowledge, in distinction from mere natural, intellectual knowledge. It is knowledge of the heart, rather than of the head. It is experimental rather than theoretical knowledge of the God of our salvation in Christ. It is personal rather than abstract. I do not make this distinction in order to disparage doctrinal knowledge of Christ. On the contrary, without intellectual knowledge of what God has revealed to us, spiritual knowledge is impossible. But mere theology is not sufficient unto salvation. One may know all *about* Christ without knowing Him. Saving knowledge of Jesus is to behold Him as the fulness of our emptiness, as the true water and bread of life which we need, as the light in our darkness, as the resurrection that is able to overcome our death. It is a personal knowledge of Him as the One that is made unto us of God wisdom, righteousness, sanctification, and redemption. It is such a knowledge of the Christ as causes us to realize that we are deeply concerned with Him, and that to possess Him is a question of life and death.

From this contrition, this sorrow according to God, this realization of our own condemnation in the judgment of God, and this true knowledge of the Saviour as the revelation of the God of our salvation, arises the third element of which we spoke, that of aspiration or longing. Seeing Him as the fulness of our emptiness, as the righteousness of God that is able to blot out all our unrighteousness, as the light that can dispel our darkness, as the life and the resurrection that is able to vanquish our death, as the bread that can satisfy our hunger and the water that can quench our thirst, we long for Him, and for all His benefits: forgiveness, the adoption unto children of God, knowledge of God, righteousness, and holiness. We hunger and thirst for Him. We want to possess Him. We cannot live without Him. We ask, we seek, we knock. For we yearn to be delivered from the guilt and the dominion of sin in order that we may have peace with God, and enter into His blessed fellowship. And as the hart panteth after waterbrooks so panteth our soul after God, after the living God as He reveals Himself in the riches of His grace in Jesus our Lord!

And this leads to the final step: appropriation of Christ and all His benefits and blessings of grace. This implies that I know with a certain knowledge that He is mine and that I belong to Him by God's unfathomable grace over me. It means that I am confident that He died for me, and that now I wash my garments in His precious blood by faith, laying hold of the forgiveness of sins, and of the righteousness of God in Him. It means that by faith I live out of Him, as He lives in me, and that I

draw out of Him grace for grace, that I eat and drink
Him, and that through Him I draw near unto God and
enter into the fellowship of His covenant. And now "I
count all things but loss for the excellency of Christ Jesus
my Lord: for whom I have suffered the loss of all things,
and do count them but dung, that I may win Christ."
Phil. 3.8.

Such are the implications of the spiritual act of coming
to Jesus. The circumstances and the manner in which
one comes to perform this spiritual act are not always the
same. Sometimes one is suddenly called out of darkness,
and he is very vividly conscious of the change whereby
he is impelled to cast himself upon the mercies of the Lord.
Thus it was with Paul on the way to Damascus. In a
moment he turned about from persecuting the Church to
acknowledge the Jesus he persecuted as his Saviour and
Lord. More often one is gradually instructed and inducted
into the knowledge of Christ from infancy, and when he
comes to years of discretion he cannot remember any particular moment when he came to Christ. Thus it must
have been with Timothy. And thus it normally is with
those that are born and brought up in the Church. But
whether in one way or another, always the act of coming
to Jesus contains the elements of contrition, spiritual knowledge, aspiration, and appropriation. Nor is the act ever
finished. Always again we come in sorrow after God, in
the acknowledgement of His fulness, with the longing and
thirst in our souls for the God of our salvation, in order
that daily we may drink of the water of life freely.

Whosoever will may come! How a sinner can thus
come to the Saviour we must consider another time. If
now it only has become plain that the will to come to
Jesus is motivated by true repentance and sorrow for sin,
is enlightened and directed by the true spiritual knowledge

of Christ as the God of our salvation, is impelled by the mighty longing after the living God and His grace, and expresses itself in appropriating Christ and all His spiritual blessings. And he that so cometh to Jesus shall never be ashamed. For He is included in the word of Christ: "All that the Father giveth me shall come to me; and him that cometh to me I will in no wise cast out." John 6:37.

Man's Coming and God's Drawing

X

Man's Coming and God's Drawing

> *No man can come to me, except the*
> *Father which hath sent me draw him.*
> —JOHN 6:44.

IT IS absolutely sure that "whosoever will may come."
And it is equally certain that whosoever comes will
certainly be received. No one was ever refused that
came to Christ to be saved. No one ever approached the
river of the water of life, thirsty and faint, and was denied
a drink. Whosoever comes to eat of the bread of life
will not be sent away hungry. One that will come to
Christ does not have to hesitate. He need not fear that
he will be disappointed or ashamed. If one asks he shall
receive. He that seeketh shall surely find. To him that
knocks it surely shall be opened. On this you may depend.
Such is the gospel. And the gospel is the promise of God
that can never fail. And this promise of the gospel is
so indubitably sure to every one that comes to Christ,
because before one can ever come to Him, and even before
one can will to come, the grace of God already operated in
his inmost heart and wrought this will to come in him.
Grace is always first. The coming of the sinner is the
fruit of God's drawing.

And this is a matter of experience of every sinner that
is saved by grace. He that comes to Jesus experiences in
this act of coming that drawing of the marvellous and

efficacious grace of God, and that, too, in such a way that the latter is first and is the cause of the former. One that is saved will surely acknowledge this. Never will a regenerated child of God present the matter of his salvation as having had its initiative in him. Never will he say that anything on his part preceded the operation of God's grace in him, that he first willed to come and God's grace thereupon enabled him to come, that he first accepted Christ and thereupon Christ received him, that he first opened his heart and thereupon Christ entered it. An unmistakable proof of this may be found in the prayer of one that is saved. Here all Arminianism, all boasting of free will in the matter of salvation, is silenced. The reason is that in prayer one speaks to God. Before men one may talk of coming to Jesus as if it were in the power of the sinner to come or to refuse to come. But as soon as one places himself before the face of God all this is changed. Then all is attributed to divine grace. Before the face of God there is no Arminian. Or whoever heard anyone utter an Arminian prayer like this: "I thank thee God that Thou didst wait until it pleased me to come, and that Thou didst knock until I was good enough to open my heart for Thee, and that Thou gavest me grace when I decided to receive it?" Yet why should not a man express before the face of God what he loudly and boldly proclaims to man? The simple answer is: because before God we cannot lie! Hence, in prayer a saved sinner will attribute all to God and none to self. He will cease speaking about the free will of man, and say: "I thank Thee that Thy irresistible grace overpowered all my resistance, that Thou didst open and enter into my heart, that Thou didst draw me that I might come!" And this is the heart of the assurance and boldness of the sinner as he comes to Jesus. The very fact that in his coming to Jesus the sinner experiences the drawing of the Father is his guarantee that he will surely be received.

And this is the clear teaching of Holy Writ.

Through the prophet Jeremiah, Jehovah says to His people Israel: "Yea, I have loved thee with an everlasting love: therefore with lovingkindness have I drawn thee." Let us not overlook that the drawing of Jehovah is presented here as an act of God's lovingkindness or mercy; and, secondly, that this act is rooted in, and a manifestation of the everlasting love of God to His people. Jer. 31:3. And what is the result of this drawing of God's love? This, "that the watchmen upon the mount Ephraim shall cry, Arise ye, and let us go up to Zion unto the Lord our God." vs. 6. The will to come to the God of our salvation is the fruit of the drawing of God. To the murmuring multitude in Capernaum, who were about to depart from Him, the Lord Jesus speaks the well-known words: "No man can come to me, except the Father which hath sent me draw him: and I will raise him up at the last day. It is written in the prophets, And they shall be all taught of God. Every man therefore that hath heard, and hath learned of the Father, cometh unto me." Let us pause a moment to consider this important passage. It teaches us first of all, that the drawing of God's grace is indispensable to the coming of the sinner. Without this drawing by the Father, it is impossible for any man to come: No man *can* come, except the Father draw him. And this does not mean, of course, that a sinner may desire, may earnestly long to come to Jesus, but that he is withheld by some constraining power, but that he has neither the will nor the power to come. The coming and the will to come are utterly dependent on the gracious drawing of the Father. Secondly, this passage explains the drawing by the Father as a being taught of God, the result of which is that a man hears and learns of the Father. You readily understand, of course, that this does not refer to the outward preaching of the Word by man. The outward preaching of the gospel by no means causes the whole audience to hear and to learn of the Father, still less to come to Christ. But the Lord here speaks of a being taught of God, of a spiritual illumination that results in a spiritual knowledge of sin, of God, of Christ, of the things concerning salvation, and that results in the spiritual act of coming to Christ. And, finally, let us note, too, that the fruit of this drawing and divine teaching is sure and infallible, for "Every man therefore that hath heard and learned of the Father cometh unto me." John 6:44, 45.

Whosoever will may come! For every man that will come has been taught to will and to come by the efficacious drawing power of the grace of God. He will surely be received.

The same truth is repeated in another form in vs. 65 of the same chapter of the gospel according to John: "And he said: Therefore said I unto you, that no man can come unto me, except it were given unto me of my Father." The same impossibility, the same utter incapability of the natural man to come to Jesus is expressed here as in the forty-fourth verse. How shall he come to Christ? Can the mere preaching of the gospel persuade him? But the preaching of the cross concerns spiritual things, and he is natural, and "the natural man receiveth not the things of the Spirit of God: for they are foolishness to him: neither can he know them, because they are spiritually discerned." I Cor. 2:14. Hence, it must be given unto him of the Father. The will and the power to come to Jesus are gifts of grace. And therefore the Lord can say triumphantly even in the face of the fact that the bread-seeking multitude of Capernaum oppose Him, and will presently apostatize from Him: "All that the Father giveth me shall come to me; and him that cometh to me I will in no wise cast out! vs. 37.

But what is this drawing of the Father through which the sinner comes to Christ?

Let me answer, first of all, in a general way, that it is a spiritual operation of God's grace, through Jesus Christ and by the Spirit of Christ, by means of the gospel, in our inmost hearts, whence are the issues of life, affecting the entire man with mind and will and all his emotions and desires. We are drawn by the Father, but that this drawing does not take place without Christ as the Mediator of our salvation, is plain from what the Lord declared shortly before His death on the cross: "And I, if I be lifted up from the earth, will draw all (men) unto me." John 12:32. Through the cross the Lord was lifted up into glory of the resurrection, and into the height of His position at the right hand of God. And as the Head of His Church He received the promise of the Spirit, in order that by that Spirit He might draw all His own unto Him into glory. The Father draws, and Christ draws also, not as if these were two separate operations, but so, that the Father draws us through Jesus Christ as the Mediator of our redemption.

And in this drawing, just as in the act of coming to Jesus, we may distinguish four steps or elements. The first step one takes in coming to the Saviour is that of contrition, true sorrow after God; and corresponding to this true sorrow over sin on the part of the sinner, is the divine act of conviction of sin. The latter is the cause of the former. Only the man that is brought under conviction of sin by the Spirit of Christ can come to true contrition and penitence. The Father draws, the sinner comes: this means, therefore, first of all, that the Father convicts, the sinner repents. This must not be confused with that other operation of God in the conscience of every sinner, whereby He inscribes into his consciousness the sentence of his guilt and condemnation, and causes him to assume responsibility for it. Every man feels that he is responsible before God for his sin. Not for a moment can he rid himself of this sense of accountability. And every sinner is convinced that he stands condemned in judgment before God. And this, too, is the work of God through His Spirit. Even the Gentiles have the work of the law written in their hearts, so that their conscience bears witness, Rom. 2:15; and the Spirit convicts the world of sin, because they believe not on Christ, John 16:9. But this is a consciousness of sin that is characterized by nothing but fear and terror, and that causes the sinner to flee from the face of Him that sitteth on the throne, and to call to the mountains and rocks to cover him. The conviction of sin unto salvation, however, is principally different. It is a conviction of love. And to be sure, the fruit also of this saving conviction is that the sinner fears and trembles before the majesty of a righteous God, yet so, that he does not flee away, nor attempt to hide himself, but rather approaches Him in true sorrow that he has offended this holy God, and taking God's side in his own condemnation, he prays in the love of God, even though it be with fear and trembling: "Search me, O God, and know my heart: try me, and know my thoughts: and see if there be any wicked way in me." Ps. 139:23, 24. This saving conviction of sin is not the work of a preacher; it is not the work of the sinner himself; it is the work of God's sovereign grace alone. And without it, the sinner

will never take the first step on the way to Jesus. No
man can come to Jesus, except the Father draw him!

The second step the sinner takes in coming to Jesus is
that of recognition, whereby the sinner beholds Christ
as the God of his salvation, as the fulness of his own
emptiness, the righteousness that is able to blot out his
own unrighteousness, the life that overcomes his death.
And corresponding to this act of spiritual recognition on
the sinner's part, is God's act of spiritual illumination,
whereby He reveals His Son unto the sinner. When He
convicts a man of sin, He does not leave him in the despair
of his condemnation: He shows him Jesus in all the fulness
of His salvation. This spiritual illumination is not the
same as that natural enlightenment whereby the sinner
knows all about Christ, even recognizes and acknowledges
to an extent by his natural powers the beauty of Christ
as the best of men, as one that was deeply God-conscious,
as a great teacher and wonderful example; but he does
not behold Him as the righteousness of God, and the cross
is foolishness to him. The Christ of the Scriptures he
crucifies afresh. Modernism in all its manifestations is
a good illustration of this. The natural man does not
understand the things of the Spirit; "they are foolishness
to him, neither can he know them, because they are
spiritually disconcerned." I Cor. 2:14. Nor does the mere
preaching of the gospel give him this spiritual knowledge
of Christ. The Lord Jesus, reviewing the result of His
own preaching gives thanks to the Father that He has
hid these things from the wise and from the prudent,
and revealed them unto babes, Matt. 11:25; and he
emphasizes that no man knoweth the Father, save the
Son, and to whomsoever the Son will reveal Him, Matt.
11:27. But when the Father draws us, He reveals unto

us Jesus in all His power of salvation. He so illumines our understanding that we behold Him as the One that is desirable above all things, as the One we need as our Redeemer and Deliverer from sin and death. He opens our eyes so that we behold Him in all the riches of His grace, in all the fulness of His righteousness and life. He opens our ears, so that we hear the Word of the cross as a power of God unto salvation. The drawing power of God causes us to seek Him as the beautiful Saviour, the God of our salvation!

However, The Father, through the Spirit of Christ, not only affects our understanding, so that we discern the Saviour spiritually, He also wonderfully operates by the same Spirit upon our will and all our desires, so that we long for Him, and desire to possess Him. This longing or aspiration, we said in another connection, is the third step in the sinner's coming to Christ. And corresponding to this yearning for Christ is the third element in the drawing of the Father, which we may call allurement or attraction. The natural man is not attracted by the Christ and His righteousness. He is carnal, and minds carnal things. The carnal mind is enmity against God. His will is perverse, and all his desires are impure. He does not hunger and thirst after righteousness. Nor can mere preaching of the gospel create such a desire after righteousness and the forgiveness of sin. But when the Father draws, and by the power of His grace marvellously operates upon the will of the sinner, He changes that will, turns it completely around, instills into the heart new desires, so that the sinner longs for righteousness, for the remission of sin, for fellowship with the living God, for His love and mercy. And as he beholds Christ as the only way unto the Father, he yearns with a strong desire to possess

Him, and to be able to say: "My Jesus, I love Thee; I know Thou art mine!"

And so, it is also due to the drawing power of the Father, through the Spirit of Christ, that the sinner finally takes the last step to come to Jesus, that of appropriation. Corresponding to this act on the sinner's part is the operation of God's grace, which the Scripture calls *sealing.* For we are "sealed with the holy Spirit of promise.' Eph. 1:13. It is by the Spirit of Christ, the Spirit of promise, that the promise of God, the promise of redemption, of rest, of satisfaction, of forgiveness, of righteousness and life, is given unto us personally, so that we are assured that this promise of God is for us. It is by this Spirit that the love of God, i. e., not our love to Him, but His love to us, revealed in the death of His Son, is shed abroad in our hearts, so that we are confident that Christ died for us, and that not only unto others, but also unto us personally, He gives the remission of sin and life everlasting. And so we are assured that Christ is ours, and that we may appropriate Him and all His benefits unto ourselves, and we are bold to confess with the Heidelberg Catechism, question one, that it is our only comfort in life and death, that we are not our own, but belong to our faithful Jesus Christ!

Thus we understand why it is so absolutely sure that "whosoever will may come." In the will to come and the coming the sinner experiences the drawing power of God's grace. God convicts him of sin, and he repents; God enlightens him by His Spirit, and He beholds the Christ in all His beauty of salvation; God allures and attracts, and he longs for the God of his salvation; God seals him, and he appropriates the Christ and all His benefits. How then could he ever be cast out? They that thus come to Jesus shall never be ashamed!

Coming and Preaching

XI

Coming and Preaching

> *How shall they believe in him of whom*
> *they have not heard?* —ROM. 10:14.

THE coming of the sinner to Jesus, which implies the will to come to Him, is the fruit of that gracious operation of the Father upon the heart and mind and will and all the desires of the sinner which the Scriptures designate by the word *drawing*. By the drawing of the Father the sinner is convicted of sin, enlightened with spiritual knowledge, attracted to Christ, and sealed by the Spirit of promise. And this marvellous operation is performed in a way that passes our understanding by the Holy Spirit as the Spirit of Christ.

However, this drawing of the sinner by which he is enabled to come to the Saviour, to embrace Him, and to appropriate all the blessings of salvation, is accomplished through the preaching of the gospel. Without the gospel, no man can come to Christ. For, first of all, the Christ to Whom the sinner must come unto salvation is revealed in, and presented by the gospel as it is contained and preserved in the Holy Scriptures. Another Christ than that of the Scriptures there is not. Without the gospel, therefore, there is no knowledge of Him, and without knowledge of the Saviour the sinner can have no contact with Him. All other things being equal, he is the richer Christian, who has the richer and fuller knowledge of the

Christ of the Scriptures. It is by increasing in knowledge that a Christian grows in grace. The preaching of the gospel, therefore, is the means through which the Father draws us to Christ. This is implied in the words of John 6:44, 45: "No man can come to me, except the Father which hath sent me draw him . . . It is written in the prophets, And they shall be all taught of God. Every man therefore that hath heard and hath learned of the Father, cometh unto me.' This hearing, and teaching, and learning, takes place through the preaching of the gospel. And this is also plainly expressed in Rom. 10:14: "How then shall they call on him in whom they have not believed? and how shall they believe in him (of) whom they have not heard? and how shall they hear without a preacher?"

Besides, the drawing operation of grace is never such that it violates the rational and moral nature of the sinner that is drawn to Jesus. It is not a compelling action. The sinner is not forced to Christ against his will and without his understanding. On the contrary, by this operation the sinner is made willing. He is so overpowered by the irresistible grace of God, that he becomes very willing to come, and that he himself makes the conscious and willing choice to turn to the God of his salvation. His will is not destroyed by grace, but turned about; his mind is not set aside, but spiritually enlightened. He is taught of God. But for this very reason the preaching of the gospel is an indispensable means. While God through the Spirit draws the sinner from within, He calls him through the gospel, and thus the sinner performs the act of coming to the Saviour consciously and willingly.

From this it will be evident how highly important it is for the Church of Christ in the world to understand, and to be faithful to her one and sacred calling: to preach the Word! For the preaching of the Word is the divinely instituted means through which it pleases God in Christ to draw sinners unto Him. To be drawn unto Christ, sinners must hear *His* voice, His own Word to them personally. They must hear Him. Nothing less will do unto salvation. The word of a man, even though he should derive the contents of his speech from the Scriptures, is not sufficient: the sinner must hear the Word of *God* The word of man is powerless, only the Word of God is with power. It alone is "quick, and powerful, and sharper than any twoedged sword, piercing even to the dividing asunder of soul and spirit, and of the joints and marrow, and is a discerner of the thoughts and intents of the heart." Heb. 4:12. Only the Word of God is efficacious: it brings to pass that which it expresses. God alone calls the things that are not as if they were. His mighty Word alone quickens the dead. When He says "Let there be light," there is light. When Christ, standing at the grave of Lazarus, calls: "Lazarus, come forth," the dead does come out of his grave. John 11:43, 44. When Christ Himself says: "Come unto Me," the sinner surely comes. That Word He alone can speak. No word of man can take its place. And it is absolutely necessary that the sinner hear that Word. For thus the Lord declares: "The hour is coming and now is, when the dead shall hear the voice of the Son of God: and they that hear shall live." John 5:25. And again: "My sheep hear my voice, and I know them, and they follow me." John 10:27. And in Rom. 10:14 the apostle Paul writes: "How shall they believe in Him whom (not: *of whom*) they have not heard?"

How could it be different? How could a word of man, how could all the begging of a preacher, ever take the place of this mighty Word of Christ unto the salvation of a sinner? How could anyone believe in the Lord Jesus Christ, except through and upon His own Word? To come to Jesus is to believe in Him. And to believe in Him is an act of absolutely certain, positive, spiritual knowledge, together with a most perfect and implicit confidence in Him as the ground and implication of my righteousness and salvation. By faith I cast myself upon Him for life and death, for time and eternity. By faith I am righteous in the midst of sin. By faith I live in the midst of death. By faith I hope in the midst of despair. By faith I am unspeakably happy in the midst of misery. By faith I contradict and am victorious over all the things of my present experience: guilt, damnation ,death, the wrath of God, hell and the devil; and I am confident that I am justified, that I live, that I am the object of God's favor, that I am heir of everlasting life and glory. And all this is true, because I believe in Christ!

But how shall a sinner perform such an act of faith? Can such faith rest upon the word of a mere man, even though he should speak about Jesus? Or can the mere word of a man create such marvellous faith in the heart of a sinner, spiritually dead, perverse of will, corrupt in heart, darkened in his understanding? I tell you nay! For such a faith nothing less than the certainty that I heard Him, Christ, the Son of God Himself, speak to me personally, can serve as a ground. Such a faith can be wrought in me only by His own Word, spoken by Himself! I must hear the Word of God! I must hear the voice of the Good Shepherd! I must hear the voice of Jesus say to me: "Come unto me, and rest.' His own Word must reach out to me, and I must hear Him call me: "Come and drink." He must Himself stand by my spiritual grave, and call: "Come forth, and rise from the dead!" Then, and then only, can I cast myself upon Him, rely on Him, come to Him, lean on His bosom, and find the promised rest.

Now, it pleases Christ to speak this mighty Word by which He draws men to Him *through the preaching.* The Word of Christ does not come to us by an inner voice, which He immediately, directly, and mystically addresses to our hearts. On the contrary, the apostle writes in that same fourteenth verse of Romans 10: "how shall they hear without a preacher?" Christ instituted the preaching of the gospel as a means whereby it pleases Him to draw His own unto Him, and to speak His Word unto them. And from this truth follow a few important points with regard to the preaching of the Word, to which I must briefly call your attention.

First of all, it is important to emphasize that preaching is ministry of the Word of God in Christ. And that denotes that it stands entirely in the service of that Word. It is and wants to be a *means* for the mighty and irresistible Word of Christ Himself to go forth. If you remember this, you will realize immediately that it is a deeply serious matter to listen to the preaching of the Word. You go to church, not to hear "a nice sermon," not to be entertained by splendid oratory, not to discover the opinion of a certain learned man on a subject, but to hear the Word of Christ addressed to you by Him. And that is a matter of life and death. For this is the essential thing in true preaching, that which distinguishes preaching from mere lecturing, that Christ Himself speaks to you through the word of him that officiates as a preacher. If Christ does not speak, there is no preaching. All the wisdom of the world, all the glittering oratory of a wonderfully fluent and attractive speaker, all the sentimentalism of a

modern revivalist, all the touching stories he may be able
to tell, all his emotional begging and pleading, are vain.
What matters, as you and I listen to the preaching of
the Word, is that we hear the voice of Jesus say: "Come
unto me, and rest," that we hear Him call: "repent and
believe," that we hear Himself assure us: "Thy sins are
forgiven thee, go in peace." Unto this end preaching is
a *means*.

Secondly, it follows that a preacher, as far as the contents of his message is concerned, is bound to his mandate
as contained in the Holy Scriptures. A preacher has no
message of his own to deliver. He is an ambassador of
Christ. And as an ambassador he must deliver the message with which he is charged by Him that sent him.
One who occupies the place of a preacher, and pretends
to be a minister of the Word, but who disregards this
mandate and delivers his own philosophy on various topics
pertaining to this world, is a false prophet. And the
Church that is unfaithful to her calling, and that, instead
of preaching the pure Word of God according to the
Scriptures, presses its pulpit into the service of the world
and its humanistic philosophy, is an abomination to Jehovah.
She is like Jerusalem of old that killed the prophets, and
that, when through these prophets Christ would gather
her children, as a hen gathereth her chicks under her wings,
would not serve that purpose, but opposed Him, and
wantonly devoured the people of God. O, Christ will
surely gather His people! Jerusalem's children will not
perish. But the judgment upon wicked Jerusalem, that
while supposed to be subservient to this purpose of gathering
Jerusalem's children, scatters them, will be terrible. And the
modern church, that proclaims the philosophy of man instead
of the Word of God, and the gospel of Jesus Christ and
Him crucified, and feeds its peoples stones for bread, is

the culmination of the false prophet, the servant of Antichrist, that with the devil and the beast will be cast into the lake that burns with fire and sulphur!

When one considers the condition of what is known as the Church in the world today, she presents a sorry spectacle indeed! It seems that by far the greater part of her has forsaken the truth of the gospel. When one happens to be in a strange place on the sabbath, far away from his home church, and enters one of the buildings that by their style of architecture suggest that it is dedicated to the ministry of the Word, and he is hungry for the bread of life, he will be bitterly disappointed in by far the majority of cases. Instead of bread he is offered stones. The Bible is, indeed, still on the pulpit. And presently, there appears in that pulpit a man who is clad in the robe of a minister of the Word, but who, when he opens his mouth to speak, becomes at once revealed as a deceiver who wholly ignores his calling, and corrupts the Word of God. And withal he makes the impression of a silly ass, for usually he is but poorly acquainted even with the philosophy he presents with a show of learning. The Church that neglects her calling to preach the Word of God is like the salt that has lost its savor: it is good for only the dunghill.

All the more reason this why the true Church of Christ should be faithful and diligently watch and be vigilant that the pure Word of God be proclaimed by her and in her midst, whether it be in her public worship or by those that preach the Word, the whole Word of God, the full counsel of God. She must preach the gospel. And the gospel is the promise, the sure promise of God. And the promise of God is Christ in all His fulness of salvation. Christ, the incarnated Son of God, the revelation of the

God of our salvation, Who was delivered for our transgressions, and raised for our justification; the Christ of
God, through Whom God actually reconciled us unto Himself, and by Whom He regenerates us, justifies us, forgives
our sins, adopts us unto His children, preserves us unto
the end, and glorifies us with Christ in the final resurrection;
Christ, Who receives all that come unto Him, not by
themselves but through the grace of the Father that draws
them, and Who surely gives drink to the thirsty, bread
to the hungry, rest to the weary, beauty for ashes, glory
for shame, life to the dead,—that Christ is the contents
of the gospel. And that Word of Christ concerning Himself the preacher must proclaim. He dare not present it
as a mere offer to all men, the reception of which depends
on the whim of man's will; He may not preach a mere
possibility of salvation: the promise of the gospel is the
promise of the living God, and the promise of God is
faithful and sure. Salvation is not a chance: it is a certainty. God Himself, not by the will of the sinner, but
in spite of his unwillingness, realizes it. That Christ, and
that promise of the gospel, sure for all that repent and
believe, that hunger and thirst, that labor and are weary
and heavy laden, the preacher must proclaim. And the
fruit of it he may and must leave to God, Who alone is
able to save, and Who is merciful to whom He will be
merciful, while whom He will he hardens.

To this must be added, finally, that a preacher must be
sent. For "how shall they preach except they be sent?"
Nor is there anything very dark or mysterious about this
calling and mission of the preacher. For through the
apostles, Christ commissioned His Church in the world
to preach the gospel. "Go ye into all the world, and preach
the gospel to every creature," is a commission, not to

any individual, but to the apostles, and through them to the Church they represented. The Church is "the pillar and ground of truth." To the Church is given the promise that the Spirit will lead her into all the truth. To the Church the Lord entrusted His Word. The Church must preserve, interpret, confess, preach the Word of life. Hence, while the Church fulfills this calling through the ministry of the Word, a preacher must be called and sent by the Church. Not the individual believer can be a preacher on his own initiative: he must be sent. Not all kinds of groups, schools, societies, boards, sects, often functioning apart from the Church, and speaking of her in deprecating language frequently, but the Church is commissioned to preach, and she alone can send and call the preacher. For that reason, the preacher will not pride himself on being "undenominational;" nor will he try to introduce all kinds of strange and new doctrines. On the contrary, he will feel himself called by the Church, and connected with the Church of all ages, will proclaim the gospel of Christ as confessed by that Church that was led by the Spirit into all the truth.

Through that preaching Christ will speak His own Word of power, and draw His own unto Him. I say: His own. For not all that outwardly hear the gospel are drawn by the Father. It is not of him that willeth, nor of him that runneth, but of God that sheweth mercy. There are always those that will be hardened, to whom the precious corner stone is a stone of stumbling, and a rock of offense. But His own He surely calls. And they surely come to Him. And He surely receives them. For His sheep hear His voice, and they follow Him, and He gives them eternal life, and they shall never perish. No one can ever pluck them out of His hand!

God's Drawing and Man's Responsibility

XII

God's Drawing and Man's Responsibility

*Nay but, O man, who art thou that re-
pliest against God?*   —Rom. 9:20.

WE have been emphasizing the truth of the statement
that "whosoever will may come," and have repeatedly
laid stress on the truth that there never was or will be a
sinner willing to come to Jesus who finds the way barred,
or who feels that he is restrained from approaching and
appropriating Him and all His blessings of salvation. On
the other hand, we also have been placing due emphasis
on the truth that no man has of himself the will to come to
Christ, and that no mere human persuasion can cause
that will to arise in his soul. In as far as the hymn from
which we derive our theme intends to convey the notion
that it is in the power of every man to will to accept Christ,
it is certainly false, calculated to instill into the hearts and
minds of men the poison of Pelagianism. Salvation is not
of him that willeth, nor of him that runneth, but of God
that sheweth mercy, Rom. 9:16. The will to come is the
fruit of the drawing of the Father. And the number of
the "whosoever will" is therefore limited to those whom it
pleases the Father to give to Christ, to give them a new
heart, and to call them out of darkness into His marvellous
light. And preceding this drawing of the Father, there
is no saving activity on the part of the sinner whatever.

This, you understand, takes the matter of salvation entirely out of the hands of the sinner, and leaves it absolutely to God. Salvation is a divine work from beginning to end. It is just as absolutely a work of God alone as is the work of creation. In no sense does man cooperate with God in his own salvation. God alone determines who shall be saved, and God alone accomplishes the work of salvation. Salvation is of the Lord. In the ultimate sense of the word, therefore, the will to come to Christ is rooted in, and is the outcome of God's unconditional, free and sovereign election of His own unto eternal life.

This truth, that God determines sovereignly who shall be saved, and who shall not be saved, the doctrine that God is GOD, that He is the sovereign Lord, even in the matter of the salvation and damnation of man, is not according to the flesh, and does not meet with general approval. How could it find grace in the eyes of sinful men? It humbles all the pride of man. It casts him prostrate in the dust. In relation to God it makes him a mere nothing. It presents him as he truly is, as less than a drop of the bucket and the dust of the balance. It leaves him no power, no wisdom, no goodness, no glory whatever. And it exalts God as the only sovereign Lord, Who is in the heavens, and Who doeth whatsoever He pleaseth, Who forms the light, and creates darkness, Who makes peace, and creates evil, Isaiah 45:7; Who is the Potter, while we are the clay, and Who forms, according to His good pleasure, vessels unto honor, and vessels unto dishonor. Rom. 9:21; and Who declares unto Pharaoh: "Even for this same purpose have I raised thee up, that I might shew my power in thee, and that my name might be declared throughout all the earth," Rom. 9:17. How could it even be expected that this doctrine that exalts God and lays low all the pride of man, could find favor

with sinful men, that always exalt themselves against the
living God?

Many objections are, and always have been raised against
this truth, and we shall not discuss them all. There is,
however, one objection that is as old as the truth itself,
one that is supposed to expose the doctrine that salvation
is of the Lord as both horrible and absurd, and which we
may well examine for a moment. It is the well-known
argument that the doctrine of God's absolute sovereignty in
the matter of salvation implies a denial of man's responsibility. If salvation is so absolutely the work of God that
He alone determines it, and that man of himself can do
nothing towards his own redemption and deliverance from
sin, then, thus runs the objection, the sinner is no longer
a moral agent, and God cannot justly hold him responsible
in the day of judgment. The doctrine of God's sovereignty
and man's responsibility stand in opposition to each other.
They involve a contradiction. And, therefore, they cannot
be true.

What shall we say in answer to this objection?

First of all, I would like to repeat that the objection is
a very old one, and that it has always been raised against
the truth of God's sovereign dealings with men in the
matter of salvation. You may study the history of the
Church and her doctrine, and you will discover that the
principal objection of the opponents to the doctrine of
absolutely sovereign grace was always the same. Always
they accused those, who faithfully proclaimed this fundamental truth, that they made God the author of sin, and
that they denied the responsibility of man. We may find
comfort in this. In this very indictment, if brought against
us, we may find a proof that we are preaching the truth.
This is especially of force, in view of the fact that the

same accusations were lodged against the apostle Paul, and that, therefore, this very objection is raised directly against the truth as revealed in the Scriptures. For in the ninth chapter of the Romans the apostle Paul is setting forth this same truth of God's sovereignty in the matter of salvation and damnation of the sinner. And there he meets two objections, which he knows will be and are being raised against this doctrine. The first is expressed in the question: "Is there unrighteousness with God?" And the second, denying the responsibility of man, is raised in the words: "Why doth he yet find fault? For who hath resisted His will?" If, therefore, one proclaims a gospel against which these objections are not raised, he may well draw the conclusion that there is something wrong with his preaching; while on the other hand, those whose preaching causes these objections to be raised, may find comfort in the fact that they are in good company.

Secondly, I want to call your attention to the fact that the apostle Paul in the face of these objections does not apologize, does not withdraw one word of what he had written with regard to God's sovereignty in the matter of salvation. He does not answer that the objector had misunderstood his meaning, and that his objection was due to a misapprehension of his teaching. O, it is very evident that the objector understood the apostle as having taught God's unconditional predestination. Only on this supposition have the objections any sense at all. An Arminian preacher, one that presents salvation as depending on the sinner's free will, does not meet with these objections. No, the apostle had been teaching that salvation is not of him that willeth, nor of him that runneth, but of God that sheweth mercy; and that, according to His sovereign good pleasure, God is merciful to whom He will be merciful, and whom He will He hardeneth. It is to this doctrine that the twofold objection is raised: then there is unrighteousness with God; and then man is not responsible, for no one can resist his will. And if the objection had been due to a misunderstanding, the apostle could easily have removed the difficulty. In that case he would have modified his statements, and we would have found in the ninth chapter of the Romans something like the following: "But my dear man, you misunderstand me. You misconstrue my words. I certainly did not intend to convey the idea that God is sovereign even over the will of man; on the contrary, His sovereignty is limited by the will of man. He hardens only those that resist His sincere efforts to save them; and He saves whosoever will be saved." Surely, some such statement on the part of the apostle would have removed the very reason for the opponent's objection. But since the apostle writes nothing of the kind, it is evident that he concedes that the opponent had understood him correctly. In Romans 9 the doctrine of unconditional predestination is taught, and not the Arminian conception. Salvation is absolutely of the Lord. To this we will hold on the basis of Scripture, regardless of any possible objection by opponents.

Thirdly, I would like to point out that the apostle does not for one moment modify his teaching, by appealing to "another side" of this doctrine. He does not shift to "another track." This is often done by those who claim to believe in God's absolutely sovereign grace, and that exactly to meet the objections raised in Romans 9. They try to maintain a double faced theology. They profess to believe in the truth of absolute predestination and of God's sovereignty in the matter of salvation. But if the objection is raised that by this doctrine they violate the

freedom of man and destroy his responsibility, they shift
to another track. They say, that although it is true that
God chose those that shall be saved, before the foundation
of the world, and that He certainly saves them, yet, He
also sincerely wills that all men shall be saved. They
profess to believe that atonement is limited, and that Christ
died only for the elect, yet, on the other hand, they also
insist that God sincerely and well-meaningly offers salvation to all men. They admit that the sinner is dead in
sin, and that of himself he cannot come to Christ, yet they
preach that God sincerely, that is, with the purpose to
save him, invites that sinner to come, though He does not
give him the indispensable gift of grace that must enable
him to come. And if you object that this is a plain contradiction, and that it is quite impossible for any believer to
embrace both elements of this contradiction, they answer
that this is a deep mystery, and that one must not curiously
inquire any further into this profound truth.

Now, I like to emphasize that it should not be difficult for
any believing Christian to accept mysteries. God is great,
and we shall never comprehend Him, though by His own
revelation we may know Him. He is the eternal One, and
we are children of time. He is the infinite, and we are
finite. He is the Creator of the heavens and of the earth,
and we are mere creatures of the dust. He is the incom-
parable One, and He dwelleth in an inaccessible light.
The more we contemplate Him, the deeper the mysteries
become. Not to admit this, is to deny God! And, therefore, the believer does not claim that he can solve all
problems, least of all those that concern God's relation to
the creature. He does not deny mysteries. On the contrary, he loves them, and in the contemplation of them, he
falls down in the dust, worships and adores. But with

equal emphasis I insist that mysteries are not the same as flat contradictions, and that the latter are no mysteries, but plain nonsense. Either, God wills that all men be saved, or He does not: both cannot be true. Either, God sincerely offers a Christ that died for all men to every sinner, or He does not: to maintain both is simply impossible. Either, man has a free will to accept or reject Christ, or he is absolutely dependent upon sovereign grace: to maintain both is nonsense. And however this may be, if this double track theology were the proper answer to the opponents of God's sovereignty in the matter of salvation, we would surely find it in the ninth chapter of the epistle to the Romans. For in the strongest terms the apostle taught the truth of absolute predestination, and of God's sovereignty to save whom He will. And against this doctrine the objection was raised, that then God must be indicted of unrighteousness, and that man is without responsibility. Yet, the apostle does not point to another side of this truth. He does not apologize. He does not shift to another track. He leaves the truth to stand in all its implications.

In the fourth place, it must be pointed out that the objection that the doctrine of God's absolute sovereignty destroys man's responsibility does not hold. The two do not contradict each other. The objection is not rooted in a logical difficulty, but proceeds from a sinful, a radically wrong, a rebellious attitude against God. The objector does not know his place. He is motivated by the desire to dethrone God, and to be God instead of Him. The lie of the devil: "Ye shall be as God," blinds his eyes, distorts his view, perverts his will. Sin, enmity against God Who is really GOD makes him argue that he will not be responsible to a God that is sovereign. This is clearly evident from the answer of the Word of God to that objector: "Who art thou, O man that repliest against God?" When the Scriptures say that God is sovereign even in the matter of man's eternal destiny, that He is merciful to whom He will be merciful, it is God that speaks. And when you or I object to this that then He cannot find fault, that He cannot judge me, and that we are not responsible to Him, we are replying against Him. But if man replies against God, he is rebellious. He must be reminded of his proper place. He is mere creature, and God is GOD! Man is a mere speck of dust one wipes off the balance, a mere drop of water that falls from the bucket. Nay, he is less than that. And if he will only understand his proper position and acknowledge it, he will no longer reply against God, nor will he foolishly argue that God's sovereignty eliminates his responsibility. On the contrary, he will understand that the greater God becomes the more he becomes responsible to the sovereign Lord of heaven and earth. Man's responsibility in relation to God's absolutely sovereign dealings is a mystery, to be sure. I cannot fathom it. It is too deep for me. But it is no contradiction. The objection is foolish.

What is responsibility? It is the state in which I am under obligation to God. And man is for ever under obligation to love the Lord his God with all his heart, and with all his soul, and with all his strength. It is the state in which man stands in judgment before God, and is answerable to Him for his deeds. And that answerability God never destroys. Whether He hardens a man or irresistibly draws him by His grace and saves him, God always deals with man as a rational moral being. When he stands in judgment before God, and is called to account for his sin, the most hardened sinner will have to admit that he sinned because he loved iniquity and hated God and His righteousness, and that, therefore, he is worthy of damnation. When through the gospel he was called to repentance, he refused. When through the same gospel he was brought into contact with Christ, he would have none of Him and crucified Him afresh. And yet, with all his sin and rebellion against God he can only be subservient to God's sovereign counsel. God is the Lord, not man. Nor is it thus that the sinner is not conscious of this absolute Lordship of God. On the contrary, his own responsibility and the absolute sovereignty of God are indelibly written in his consciousness. And even in hell all the devils and ungodly will forever have to admit, that they never prevailed against His will, that He is absolute Lord and does all His good pleasure, and that He is righteous when He judgeth! The voice of rebellion will then forever be silenced.

Nor, on the other hand, does God destroy a man's moral sense, when by His irresistible grace He draws him unto Christ, and makes him heir of everlasting salvation. Ask a believer why he comes to Christ, and he will answer: "because I am lost in sin, and I know it; because I repent and long for forgiveness; because I hunger and thirst after righteousness, and I see and know Christ as my only righteousness before God; because I desire to live in God's fellowship and according to His precepts, and I know that this is possible only through the grace of Christ. I want to come to Him!" Yet, ask that same believer again how he came to know and acknowledge all this, and he will answer without hesitation: "only through the sovereign, irresistible grace of God in Christ, that drew me, that gave me eyes to see and ears to hear, and

a heart to yearn after Him.   My salvation is of the Lord!"
And in heaven the redeemed children of God will for ever
walk in highest and most perfect freedom, yet they will
always acknowledge that it is not of him that willeth, nor
of him that runneth, but of God that sheweth mercy.   No
flesh will ever glory in His presence!

Coming Ever Nearer

XIII

Coming Ever Nearer

> *But grow in grace, and in the knowl-*
> *edge of our Lord and Saviour Jesus*
> *Christ.* —II PET. 3:18.

IN a sense, that is, principally, the spiritual act of coming
to Christ is accomplished and finished once for all the
moment one has appropriated Christ and all His benefits
of salvation by a true and living faith. One does not accept
Christ piecemeal, as if one could receive first one, then
another, of the riches of Christ, until he is fully saved. On
the contrary, he that comes to Christ embraces and receives
Him in all His fulness, and all the spiritual blessings of
grace are his. In Christ he has full redemption. He does
not receive forgiveness of some sins, while other sins
are still imputed unto him, but in coming to Christ he
embraces the forgiveness of *sin,* and he is assured that no
sin can ever be imputed to him anymore. He is fully
justified before God, so that, even though his own conscience accuse him of having violated, and of still violating
all the commandments of God, yet, before God in Christ
he is accounted so righteous that he could not be more
perfectly righteous if he had never had or committed any
sin. In coming to Christ he does not receive a little life,
but he is very really raised from the dead, and is become
an heir of eternal life. For he that believeth on the Son

hath eternal life. John 3:36. From death he was translated to life, from darkness he was called to light, from a guilty and corrupt sinner he became a righteous and holy child of God. He that is in Christ is become a new creature, old things have passed away, all things have become new. II Cor. 5:17.

Nor is it possible, as far as this principle of the new life that is in him is concerned, that he should ever permanently and completely turn back and depart from Christ. A Christian's life does not consist of a series of separate acts of departing from the Saviour and returning to Him again. It may appear to him often as if this be the case. In his conscious life he does not always live in close fellowship with the Lord. Besides, he may fall into sin, and for a time it may seem to him as if his relationship to Jesus were completely severed. But in principle this is never tbe case. It might, nay, it surely would be so, he surely would lose his hold upon the Christ, if even for a moment his abiding in Christ depended on his will and power. But even as his coming to Jesus is but the fruit of the Father's drawing by the Spirit of Christ, so his abiding in Christ is the result of his being held in the almighty hand of Christ, and of the Father. For the Saviour Himself declares: "And I give unto them eternal life; and they shall never perish, neither shall any man pluck them out of my hand. My Father, which gave them me, is greater than all; and no man is able to pluck them out of my Father's hand. I and my Father are one." John 10:28-30.

And yet, in another sense, this act of coming to Jesus is never accomplished, and is never finished, even till the day of our death. When someone returns home from a far journey the act of his coming is finished as soon as he arrives. Not so the spiritual act of coming to Christ. The reason is that, although in principle the Christian is fully saved as soon as he appropriates Christ, he is still in the flesh, in his old nature, and that, too, in the midst of this present world. And all that belongs to the flesh and to the world constantly tends to draw him away from Jesus, and from the spiritual things of the kingdom of God. According to the principle of salvation that is in him by grace, he is perfectly righteous before God, justified in Christ; but according to the old man, he is still in sin, and daily he must repent and receive the forgiveness of sin. On the one hand, he rejoices that he has peace with God, yet, on the other hand, his conscience accuses him that he keeps none of God's commandments perfectly, and still violates them all. According to the new principle of life in him, he is holy, delivered from the dominion of sin; but according to the old man, he is corrupt, sold under sin. The new man in him is heavenly, but his old nature is earthy. And so we may say, indeed, that his act of coming to Jesus is never finished. It is a constant act of faith. Constantly, he departs from sin, repents, comes to Christ, seeks refuge in Him as the God of His salvation.

And again, although the believer comes to Christ once for all when he first receives and appropriates Him, yet, it is also true that he draws ever nearer to Him in the way of a normal, healthy spiritual development. His knowledge of, and sorrow over sin grows deeper; his recognition and apprehension of the riches of Christ become clearer and fuller; his need of, and his longing for the Saviour become more fervent; his appropriation of Christ and all His benefits become more assured and complete. Nearer, always nearer he draws to the full and rich Christ as

He is revealed to him in the gospel, and Christ is more
and more formed in him.

This need of the believer's constant approach to Christ,
and of his growth in grace, is strongly emphasized in
Scripture. We are admonished not to be conformed to
this world, but to be transformed by the renewing of our
mind, that we may prove what is that good, and acceptable,
and perfect will of God, Rom. 12:2. And as we behold
with open face, as in a glass, the glory of the Lord, we
are changed into the same image from glory to glory, even
as by the Spirit of the Lord, II Cor. 3:18. In Eph.
4:11-16, we are instructed that Christ "gave some, apostles;
some, prophets; some, evangelists; some, pastors and
teachers; for the perfecting of the saints, for the work of
the ministry, for the edifying of the body of Christ: till
we all come in the unity of the faith, and of the knowledge
of the Son of God, unto a perfect man, unto the measure
of the stature of the fulness of Christ: that henceforth we
be no more children, tossed to and fro, and carried about
with every wind of doctrine, by the sleight of men, and
the cunning craftiness, whereby they lie in wait to deceive;
but speaking the truth in love, may grow up in him in all
things, which is the head, even Christ: from whom the
whole body fitly joined together and compacted by that
which every joint supplieth, according to the effectual
working in the measure of every part, maketh increase
of the body unto the edifying of itself in love." For the
saints in Philippi, the apostle prays, that their love "may
abound yet more and more in knowledge and in all judgment," in order that they "may approve things that are
excellent;" and may "be sincere and without offense till
the day of Christ." Phil. 1:9, 10. And to the Church of
Colosse he writes that they must be rooted and built up

in Christ, as they have been taught, abounding therein with thanksgiving. And they must be vigilant, lest any man spoil them through philosophy and vain deceit, for in Christ alone dwelleth all the fulness of the Godhead bodily. Col. 2:7-9. Believers must therefore, as newborn babes, desire the sincere milk of the word, that they may grow thereby. I Pet. 2:2. And they must grow in grace, and in the knowledge of our Lord and Saviour Jesus Christ, II Pet. 3:18.

This growth in grace consists exactly in an ever closer approach to the Christ of the Scriptures. We must draw ever nearer to Him. He is the Head. In Him dwells all the fulness. Apart from Him we have nothing. That we are saved is only because He dwells in us. That we increase and grow in grace can only mean that He is more and more formed in us, that we become more and more like Him. We must be rooted and built up in Him. We must be changed into His image. We must come to the unity of the faith, and to the knowledge of the Son of God. We must approach ever nearer to the measure of the stature of the fulness of Christ, and we must grow up in Him who is the head, even Christ. To come ever nearer to Christ, therefore, is not a mere sentimental experience, a mystical enjoyment of salvation, a matter of blessed feeling and emotion. On the contrary, it means, on the one hand, that in ourselves we become ever more completely lost and undone, while Christ becomes ever greater and richer as the object and ground of our faith and hope; while on the other hand, He becomes more and more reflected in the beauty of His spiritual virtues in all our walk and conversation.

O, even when we first believe in Christ, we know and confess that we are sinful, lost and damnable before God. But an entire lifetime is not sufficient to reveal to us just how miserable, how corrupt, how deeply sinful we really are. As we grow in grace and draw nearer to Christ, we recognize more and more fully and deeply that we really lie in the midst of death, and that all our righteousnesses are but filthy rags. We become more spiritually sensitive. Sins we never noticed before now begin to stand out in bold relief. That which formerly we did not even consider to be sin, now becomes a matter of abhorrence and repentance. Our sorrow after God becomes more real. And as we grow in the knowledge of and sorrow over sin, Christ becomes more precious to us. We behold Him much more clearly in all the fulness and riches of His grace. We recognize Him more and more as the One that alone can fulfill our need, as our Bread and Water of life, as our Life and Resurrection. We long for Him, hunger and thirst after Him, more fervently. And the blessings of His grace, of righteousness and the forgiveness of sins, of the adoption unto children and heirs, of wisdom and knowledge, of sanctification and redemption, and of the hope of eternal life and glory, become even more precious to us. O, it is true, when we first believe in Christ, we embrace and appropriate, not a part of Him, but Himself, fully and completely, but we do not half realize what glorious riches of salvation have thus become ours. All the years of our present life are not sufficient to make us conscious possessors of those blessings of grace. We must draw ever nearer to Him, even Christ, Who is the Head, and in Whom alone all the fulness dwells.

And as we thus approach Him, draw ever closer to Him; as we thus become lost in ourselves ever more fully, that Christ may live in us by faith, we will also grow in spiritual virtues, and Christ will be more and more reflected in all our walk and conversation in the world. He will be formed in us, and will become manifest through us in the spiritual virtues of holiness, love, meekness, humility, patience, longsuffering, temperance in all things, prayer and thanksgiving. We will work out our own salvation with fear and trembling, knowing that it is God that worketh within us to will and to do of His good pleasure. We will hate sin and love righteousness, we will eschew evil and do good, we will keep our garments clean in the midst of a world of darkness and corruption, and living in spiritual separation from and antithesis to the world and its unfruitful works of darkness, represent the cause of the Son of God, walking as children of light, and willing to suffer with Him that we may also be glorified together.

Thus we draw ever nearer to Christ.

And this constant coming to Christ, like our first appropriation of Him, is the fruit of His own drawing of us through the Spirit, and by means of the gospel. The fulness of Christ is revealed in the gospel. If, therefore, we would grow in grace and draw nearer to Christ, we must increase in the spiritual knowledge of Him. And if we are to grow in the spiritual knowledge of the Saviour, we must constantly increase in the knowledge of the gospel, that is, of the Holy Scriptures. And in this connection, we must make one or two observations that are of great importance, especially for our own day.

First of all, if it be indispensable unto spiritual growth that believers increase in the knowledge of the gospel, as revealed in the Holy Scriptures, it is evident that in this respect the Church, I mean the instituted Church with its main calling in the ministry of the Word, has a great responsibility. I mean the responsibility to preach the pure and unadulterated gospel in all its fulness and implications, the whole counsel of God. She must not tolerate that on her pulpit the philosophy of man is proclaimed; she may not have patience with false doctrines; she must insist on the preaching of the pure Word of God, and nothing else. It cannot escape our attention that wherever the Scriptures speak of the growth of the believers in Christ, they also warn against false teachers, and against the philosophy of the world. By false doctrines the saints cannot grow. They are stones, not bread. According as a church begins to mix the preaching of the Word with the philosophy of carnal men, her members will become weak and frail, spiritually anemic; while, on the other hand, in the measure that she proclaims the pure gospel, and is vigilant against the intrusion of false teachers, her members will be spiritually healthy and strong, and grow in the grace and knowledge of our Lord and Saviour Jesus Christ.

But even this is not sufficient.

The preaching of the Word must not only be pure and unadulterated, it must also be rich and complete, it must comprise the whole counsel of God. The babe cannot grow strong and robust, if you always feed it milk. The time comes when it will need solid food. The same is true spiritually. The proclamation of a gospel you can write on your thumbnail is not conducive to the spiritual growth of the saints in Christ. The preaching of the Word must proclaim the full Christ as the revelation of the God of our salvation, all the mysteries of the gospel. Preaching must be expository. It must be indoctrinating. Beware of the false slogan: "Doctrine does not matter, if only the gospel is preached." It is of the devil. The Church must grow in Christ, she must be founded in the truth, she must increase in knowledge. And that means that she is in need of doctrine. And the Church, through the ministry of the Word, must thoroughly indoctrinate its members in all the knowledge of the fulness of Christ.

This also implies that every believer has the calling to seek that ministry of the Word, and diligently to attend it. It is his sacred calling to join himself to that Church in the world where the Word of God is most purely preached, and to separate himself from every manifestation of the false Church. He must not speak deprecatingly of the Church, nor despise the ministry of the Word, or imagine that he can just as well grow in grace by edifying himself at home. For it is exactly through the ministry of the Word that Christ speaks His Word and builds up His Church, and through that ministry, in the fellowship of the saints, He draws His own, and they follow Him and come ever nearer to Him.

Such is the way to spiritual increase and growth in grace. It is a way, which has been forsaken, and well-nigh forgotten by the greater part of what is called Church in our day, to its own destruction. It is a way that is despised by thousands that profess to be Christians. But it is the way nevertheless, and the only way. And we call upon the Church, and upon believers individually to return to that way, in order that we be no longer children, tossed to and fro, and carried about by every wind of doctrine, but may grow up in Him Who is the head, even our Lord Jesus Christ!

Of course, our coming to Christ is never finished in this life. Always we have but a small beginning of the new life as long as we are in the body of this death; always we know in part only, as long as we do not see face to face. The final step of our coming to Jesus we cannot take, until the earthly house of this tabernacle shall be dissolved, and we shall enter into our house of God, not made with hands, eternal in the heavens. The perfect knowledge of, and likeness to Christ, awaits us on the other side of death and the grave, in the domain of the resurrection, where He shall make our mortal bodies like unto His most glorious body, and draw us unto Himself in everlasting perfection through His final word: "Come ye, blessed of my Father, inherit the kingdom prepared for you from before the foundation of the world!" Then we shall be like Him, and see Him face to face!